The
iPhone
How to do the things you
want to do with your iPhone **Book**

Scott Kelby & Terry White

The iPhone Book

The iPhone Book Team

TECHNICAL EDITORS
Kim Doty
Cindy Snyder

TRAFFIC DIRECTOR
Kim Gabriel

PRODUCTION MANAGER
Dave Damstra

COVER DESIGN AND
CREATIVE CONCEPTS
Felix Nelson
Jessica Maldonado

STUDIO SHOTS
Scott Kelby
Rafael Concepcion

PUBLISHED BY
Peachpit Press

Composed in Myriad, Lucida Grande, and Helvetica by Kelby Publishing.

Trademarks
All terms mentioned in this book that are known to be trademarks or service marks have been appropriately capitalized. Peachpit Press cannot attest to the accuracy of this information. Use of a term in the book should not be regarded as affecting the validity of any trademark or service mark.

iPhone, iPod, iTunes, Macintosh, and Mac are registered trademarks of Apple. Windows is a registered trademark of Microsoft Corporation.

Warning and Disclaimer
This book is designed to provide information about the iPhone. Every effort has been made to make this book as complete and as accurate as possible, but no warranty of fitness is implied.

The information is provided on an as-is basis. The author and Peachpit Press shall have neither liability nor responsibility to any person or entity with respect to any loss or damages arising from the information contained in this book or from the use of the discs or programs that may accompany it.

ISBN 13: 978-0-321-53410-1
ISBN 10:   0-321-53410-7

9 8 7 6 5 4 3 2

Printed and bound in the United States of America

This seal indicates the content provided is created, and produced solely by the National Association of Photoshop Professionals (NAPP). Additionally, it ensures the content maintains the stringent standards set by NAPP, the world's leading resource for Adobe® Photoshop® training, education and news.

www.peachpit.com
www.scottkelby.com

For Barbara Stephenson, for picking
up where my mom left off.
–SCOTT KELBY

For my mom who always taught me to do the right thing
and to my dad who inspired me and pushed me to succeed.
–TERRY WHITE

Scott's Acknowledgments

This is the second book I've been lucky enough to co-author with Terry, and I can tell you from experience that the only downside of co-authoring a book with him is that you only get half as much space to thank all the wonderful people whose help, hard work and support go into making a book like this.

To Kalebra: My wonderful, amazing, hilarious, fun-filled, super-gorgeous, and loving wife. Your spirit, warmth, beauty, brains, patience, and unconditional love continue to prove what everybody always says—I'm the luckiest guy in the world.

To Jordan & Kira: You two little bundles bring immeasurable joy to my life, and I'm so proud and tickled to be your dad. I couldn't ask for anything more.

To Jeff: You are the world standard that all brothers should be judged by. No wonder everybody loves you the way they do!

To my co-author Terry White: You're the one who convinced me to do this book, and without your many ideas, your influence, and your great writing, this book would never have seen the light of day. I'm truly honored to have shared these pages with you, and to count you among my very best friends.

To Kathy Siler (my secret weapon): Without you, I'd be sitting in my office mumbling and staring at the ceiling. Thanks for doing all the "hard work," and making my work life have calm, order, and sense, and for making it all a lot of fun. You are the best.

To my editor Kim Doty: I just love working with you. How can you not love working with someone who always has such a warm smile, such a great attitude, and does such great work? Thanks doesn't cover it…but…thanks.

To Cindy Snyder, Jessica Maldonado, and Dave Damstra (my book editing, design, and layout team): I just love working with you guys, and I'm constantly impressed and amazed at the quality of what you do, and how quickly you can do it.

To Felix Nelson, my brilliant Creative Director: What can I say—you are the best in the business, and ideas and art flow out of you like a Pez dispenser. I'm a very lucky guy to even get to work with you. Thank you, my friend, for everything you do for me, and our company.

A big thanks to **RC (the Photoshop "Zorro")**, who helped immeasureably in getting the iPhone photos for this book, and also thanks to **Corey Barker** for assisting me on the lifestyle shoots.

To Dave Moser: Getting to work with my best buddy every day is definitely a blessing, but the way you're always looking out for me takes it to a whole new level. :-)

To Jean A. Kendra: Thanks for watching "the other side" of our business, and for being such a great friend over the years.

To Nancy Ruenzel, Ted Waitt, Scott Cowlin, and all my friends at Peachpit Press: Thank you for making the book-writing process virtually painless, and for having me as one of your authors (and for letting me drop books like this in at the last minute).

To John Graden, Jack Lee, Dave Gales, Judy Farmer, and Douglas Poole: Your wisdom and whip-cracking have helped me immeasurably throughout my life, and I'm both grateful and totally in your debt.

To God and His son Jesus Christ: Thank you for always hearing my prayers, for always being there when I need You, for blessing me with such a wonderful joy-filled life, and such a warm, loving family to share it with.

Terry's Acknowledgments

It's not every day that I get to work on a project that is both challenging and fun at the same time. Writing a book such as this takes a lot of focus and attention to detail. Although there were many late nights and time spent away from my family, they didn't complain once. I have an amazing wife who knows that one of my passions is technology and gadgets, so she completely understood when I said, "Hey, guess what? I'm going to co-author *The iPhone Book* with Scott!" Carla is my balance and she helps me in so many ways every day. I also have two amazing daughters: Ayoola is both smart and constantly focused on taking it to the next level. I see so much of myself in her at times that it's scary. My youngest daughter, Sala, has many of my other traits. She makes me laugh out loud every day and lives to enjoy life. They make those late nights, long weekends, and hectic travel schedules worthwhile because at the end of the day it's all for them anyway. I also have a great sister, Pam, who is the person I go to when I need advice. It's great having an older sibling and she's the best sister a guy could have.

I also have to thank all my "gadget buddies"! It's the guys and gals that I hang out with that inspire me to play and learn about gadgets of all kinds. My colleague Dave Helmly—we call him "Radar"—is probably more of a gadget freak than I am. Nine out of 10 times, when I call him to tell him about a new toy, he's already got one in his hands and starts telling me about it. My buddy Larry Becker is always calling me and letting me in on the latest gadget that he just heard about or got to play with. Also, I thank my friends at my local Apple Store: Linda, Mike, Carol, Amir, Shaun, and Dave for constantly making me feel like a VIP when I walk in. And, of course I have to thank all my friends who support me at my Macintosh users' group, MacGroup-Detroit, especially Mary, Joe, Calvin, Jack, Chita, Phyllis, Yvonne, Bill, Shirley & Shirley, Brian & Char, Loretta, Mia, Michele, Leonard, Mike, Aquil, and Harold.

Although I enjoy writing, it's not my full-time gig. I have the best job on the planet and work for the best company in the world. I have to give special thanks to my boss, Sue Scheen, who not only inspires me with her natural leadership abilities, but also gives me the freedom and the time off that I need to pursue my other technology and industry passions. I work with some of the smartest people in the industry, and I want to thank everyone at Adobe Systems, Inc., not only for providing the best software tools in existence but also for keeping me technically educated and motivated to achieve greatness.

Of course, I have to thank the guy who is probably my biggest source of inspiration, and that is one of my best friends and the co-author of this book, Scott Kelby. I'm constantly amazed at how much this guy accomplishes each year. There is no stopping him. Not only is he great in his career, but he's also a great father to his two beautiful kids and a great husband to his wonderful wife Kalebra. I probably wouldn't have gotten into all this writing if it wasn't for Scott. Scott, you're an inspiration to us all! Thanks, buddy!

About The Authors

Scott Kelby

Scott is Editor-in-Chief and Publisher of *Photoshop User* magazine, and Editor-in-Chief and Publisher of *Layers* magazine. He is President and co-founder of the National Association of Photoshop Professionals (NAPP), the trade association for Adobe® Photoshop® users, and President of the software, education, and publishing firm Kelby Media Group.

Scott is a photographer, designer, and award-winning author of more than 40 books on technology and digital imaging, including the best-selling books: *The iPod Book*, *The Digital Photography Book*, *Photoshop Down & Dirty Tricks*, and *The Photoshop Book for Digital Photographers*. Scott has authored several best-selling Macintosh books, including *Mac OS X Tiger Killer Tips*, *Getting Started with Your Mac and OS X*, and the award-winning *Macintosh: The Naked Truth*, all from New Riders, and *Mac OS X Conversion Kit* from Peachpit Press. He is also Series Editor for the *Killer Tips* books series from New Riders. His books have been translated into dozens of different languages, including Russian, Chinese, French, German, Spanish, Korean, Greek, Turkish, Japanese, Dutch, and Taiwanese, among others.

For the past three years, Scott was awarded the distinction of being the world's No. 1 best-selling author of all computer and technology books, across all categories.

Scott is Training Director for the Adobe Photoshop Seminar Tour, Conference Technical Chair for the Photoshop World Conference & Expo, and is a speaker at trade shows and events around the world. He is also featured in a series of software training DVDs, and has been training Mac and Windows users since 1993.

For more background on Scott, visit his blog at www.scottkelby.com.

Terry White

Terry is the author of *Secrets of Adobe Bridge* from Adobe Press and co-author of *InDesign CS/CS2 Killer Tips*, from New Riders.

Terry is Director of the North America Creative Pro Core Business for Adobe Systems, Inc. and has been with Adobe for over a decade, where he leads a team of solution engineers and product specialists that focus on professional publishing and Web authoring. Terry is both an Adobe Certified Expert and Creative Suite Master.

He has been active in the industry for over 20 years and is the founder and president of MacGroup-Detroit, Michigan's largest Macintosh users' group, and is a columnist for *Layers* magazine and *X-Ology Magazine*. Terry is the host of the top-ranked *Adobe Creative Suite Video Podcast* and author of the world renown Terry White's Tech Blog (http://terry white.com/techblog), and is a key presenter at major industry shows around the world.

Table of Contents

Chapter One   1

The Bare Essentials

That Stuff You Have to Learn First

Chapter Two   23

Phoneheads

How to Use the iPhone's Phone

Table of Contents

Chapter Three   61
Please Mr. Postman
Getting (and Sending) Email on Your iPhone

Table of Contents

Table of Contents

Skip This Part, It's Not For You.

Really, I should skip this part?

Well, probably, but I guess that depends. If you've had your iPhone for a few months and you already know how to turn it on, how to zoom in, how to navigate around, put it to sleep, and of course you clearly understand how each day, before you use your iPhone, you must attenuate the built in self leveling device, including the exact application of the proper amount of iPhone diopter fluid, then you can skip right to Chapter 2.

What in the world is iPhone diopter fluid?

I dunno—I made that up, but I liked that one even better than my made up "attenuate the built-in self-leveling device" line before it.

Why would you make this stuff up?

I guess that's what happens when you mix alcohol with prescription drugs.

Are you serious?

No, of course not (well, that's probably what does happen when you mix those two, but I didn't. Mix them. You know what I mean!). Anyway, here's why I did it: to get you to read this introduction. In every book I write, I have to find some trick, some ruse, some hidden device to trick people who've bought the book into reading the introduction, because nobody (especially in books that deal with any type of technology or cool gadget like an iPhone) takes the time to do that—they just want to jump right to Chapter 1, and that's really, really bad.

Why is that such a bad thing?

Because I took the time to write this, and if you don't read it, all that time goes to waste (plus, I get a small commission for each reader who reads this introduction. It's not much, but it adds up).

Seriously, how long could it have taken to write these three pages?

Okay, not that long, but if it didn't take very long to write them, then imagine how little time it would take to read them. Yet, pretty much everybody skips right over a book's introduction because (you guessed it) they can't take the time to read it. Now, the real reason I want you to read this introduction is because this is where the author (me) lets the reader know how to use the book so they get the very most out of it.

Oh, so reading it is going to help me?

Absolutely, because you'll understand how I structured the book, what to look for, who wrote what, why we wrote it, plus (and perhaps more importantly) you'll learn that, thankfully, the rest of the book isn't like this—laced with my quirky sense of humor—it's much more straight to the point. Well, except for the opening page of each chapter, which are even more "quirky" than this intro, so if that type of thing annoys you (apparently, it annoys the living daylights out of some people, and they use a different term than "quirky" to describe it), then skip right over those chapter intros and go straight to the content, because those chapter openers have little (if anything) to do with what's in the chapters themselves.

So why do you write them that way?
It's because the rest of the book is pretty much step-by-step instructions, like "tap this button" or "scroll through this screen," and there's little opportunity to inject any of the author's own personality, so I've always used those intros to sort of "be me," even though it's not many pages.

So you're really like that in person?
Sadly, yes.

So which one are you?
I'm Scott, and I wrote this introduction, along with the silly chapter introductions, and the chapters on: iPhone essentials, the iPhone applications, the iPhone's "phone," photos on your iPhone, and the basics of using iTunes. Terry wrote the chapters on: the iPhone's email, using the iPhone Safari Web browser, the iPhone's settings, how to use the iPhone's iPod, and how to troubleshoot your iPhone.

How did you decide who writes what?
I made Terry write all the really hard chapters.

So when I'm reading the book, do you make a note of who wrote what?
Besides the list of who wrote which chapter that I just gave you—no. Of course, you now know who wrote what thanks to the fact that I tricked you into reading this introduction. Now you're a more informed reader and a better all-around person because of it.

Oh, so that's why we should read the introduction?
Well, that and a lot more things. For example, as I mentioned at the beginning, if you pretty much already know the basics about your iPhone, you can skip over to Chapter 2 and start there. Also, at the bottom of many pages in the book, Terry and I have tossed in little iTips, which are little-known shortcuts, tips, suggestions, or tricks that can make using your iPhone easier or more fun.

Okay, so what's the best way to use this book?
You don't really have to read this book in order, chapter-by-chapter, because we designed it to be a "jump-in-anywhere" book, so if you want to learn how to do a certain thing, just flip over to that page and start reading. Each page in the book shows you how to do just one important thing. One topic. One idea. One feature. It's simple (kind of like the iPhone itself). For example, if you want to learn how to delete an email, we will show you, step-by-step, how to do exactly that. No big discussions about email account protocols, or about server-side instructions—just how to delete a piece of spam, that's it. We skipped the information overload and all the tech-geek jargon, and we tell you everything the

same way we would if you asked either of us to show you in person. So, when you want to learn a particular thing about your iPhone, just find the topic in the Table of Contents, turn to that page, and you'll have the answer you need in seconds. That's what makes this a "show-me-how-to-do-it" book (rather than a "tell-me-all-about-it" book). However, if at some point in the future you decide that you want to read in-depth discussions on email compression algorithms, then you can go and buy one of those 500-page "everything-known-to-man-about-the-iPhone" books.

Anything else I should know?

Nah—I think you're good for now. I do want to offer this closing thought: if after all this, you decide to go ahead and read the basics chapter (Chapter 1), don't worry—I won't tell anybody. In fact, it's entirely possible that you'll learn at least one or two little things you didn't know, or might have missed, and if that's the case, it makes it all worthwhile (plus, since the chapter is pretty short, it'll only take you a few extra minutes to read it), and now that you've already invested your time in reading this introduction, seriously—what's a few extra minutes? So, if I were you (and I am), I'd go ahead and at least skim through Chapter 1. Okay, I think you're ready. Turn to whichever chapter you feel most drawn to, and dive right in.

Come on, isn't there "one last thing"?

Oh yeah (thanks for reminding me). On behalf of Terry and myself, and the thousands of people who worked on this book (it was really more like eight but "thousands" sounds so much more impressive), thanks for taking the time to read this introduction, thanks for buying the book in the first place (unless, of course, you shoplifted it), and we genuinely hope it helps you to have more fun, and get the most out of the coolest phone ever made.

Chapter One
The Bare Essentials
That Stuff You Have to Learn First

I was originally going to name this chapter *Basic Training* after the 1985 movie by the same name (or the 1971 version of *Basic Training*, or the 2006 version which went straight to video despite the fact it starred The Rock). But I started to wonder how many people would actually read a chapter that has the word "basic" in the title. It's sad, but nobody really wants to learn the basics anymore—they want to jump into the deep end of the pool and start with some advanced techniques, because they figure the basic stuff is too basic for them. So basically, I thought instead about using the title from the movie *Basic Instinct*. Now, I never actually saw the movie myself (didn't it have Scatman Cruthers in it?), but I heard it was better than *Basic Instinct 2*, which I think starred Carrot Top and Ernest Borgnine (but since I didn't see that one either, I can't swear they were actually in it). So I started thinking of a term that meant basics but didn't have the downside of the word basics, and I came up with "essentials." Because this chapter covers the essential stuff you'll need to really make the most of your iPhone, but "essentials" has no marketing flair. No pizzaz. No bling. (No bling?) So I thought, what device do American marketers use to capture the attention of today's most coveted demographic (people with credit left on their Visa cards), and then *Bare Essentials* (from the short-lived 1991 TV series of the same name) came to mind. It sounds just naughty enough to trick someone into reading it, but not so naughty that Snoop Dogg would read it. That brings up an interesting question. What are you doing here?

1

Turning Your iPhone On

To turn on your iPhone, press the Sleep/Wake button at the top of the iPhone (shown circled here in red). After a moment the Apple logo will appear, and shortly after that you'll be greeted with the Home screen, which is pretty much your main jumping off point to all the different things the iPhone can do.

iTip

Want to keep the info on your iPhone private? Then password protect it, so each time it wakes from sleep it asks you to input your secret 4-digit password. To do this, start at the Home screen and tap on Settings. Then tap on General, and tap on Passcode Lock. Enter a 4-digit password. Don't worry—if you forget your password, you can unlock your iPhone and assign a new password by just syncing your iPhone to your computer (not any computer—your computer).

Putting Your iPhone to Sleep

If you want to put your iPhone to sleep (which is a great way to conserve battery life when you're not actively using any of the iPhone's functions), you just press the Sleep/Wake button on the top once (even though your iPhone is asleep, it will still receive calls and text messages as if it was on). When you put your iPhone to sleep, you'll hear a little click sound and your screen will go blank. While your iPhone is in this Sleep mode, the buttons on the screen are deactivated, so if you put the iPhone in your pocket (or purse) it won't accidentally come on and start playing a song, or a video, or doing anything that would waste battery time. To wake your iPhone from Sleep mode, you can either tap that button again, or press the Home button on the bottom center of your iPhone (just below the screen). When your iPhone wakes, the screen is still locked (just in case you awakened it accidentally). To unlock the screen, just press your finger lightly on the gray button with the right-facing arrow on the bottom left of the screen, slide it to the right, and the Home screen appears.

Turning Your iPhone Completely Off

If you want to turn your iPhone completely off (you won't receive phone calls or text messages), just press-and-hold the Sleep/Wake button on the top of the iPhone for a few seconds until the red Slide to Power Off button appears. To shut down, just take your finger, press lightly on that red button, and slide it to the right. Your screen will turn black, you'll see a small round status icon for just a moment, then your iPhone will power off.

Getting Stuff into Your iPhone with iTunes

The way you get music, videos, movies, your address book, calendars, photos, etc., into your iPhone is through Apple's free software called iTunes (you must have version 7.3 or higher to work with your iPhone) for Windows and Macintosh computers. Think of iTunes as the gateway between your computer and your iPhone. (*Note:* If you've been using an iPod, you already have iTunes—just make sure you have the latest update.)

Mac: If you have a Macintosh, iTunes comes preinstalled on every Mac (and has for years), so you've already got it (just make sure you have the latest version of iTunes by launching iTunes, and then going under the iTunes menu and choosing Check for Updates). When you plug your iPhone into your Mac (this is called "syncing") it automatically launches iTunes and uploads any music, videos, photos, etc., you have in iTunes right into your iPhone.

Windows: If you're a Windows user, then you'll need to go to Apple.com/itunes and download the latest version of iTunes now (remember—iTunes is free software). Once you've downloaded and installed iTunes, you'll use it to manage and sort all your music, videos, movies, etc. (including anything you buy from the iTunes Store), and you'll use it to choose which songs, videos, movies, etc., actually get uploaded into your iPhone (there's a whole chapter on just how to do this. It's Chapter 6).

Getting Back to the Home Screen

There's only one "hard" button (an actual real button you can feel) on the face of the iPhone (it's found just below the touchscreen), and it's very important because with it you're only one click away from being back at the Home screen. Just press it, and the familiar Home screen appears (okay, it might not be that familiar right now, but don't worry—it will be sooner than you'd think). From then on, you'll use the touchscreen controls for navigating around your iPhone, making calls, playing music, and pretty much everything else the iPhone does.

---

iTip

If you press-and-hold the Home button (rather than just clicking it), you can use your other hand to navigate to other areas of your iPhone, and when you finally release the button, it takes you back to the Home screen.

Charging Your iPhone

Apple gives you two ways to charge your iPhone: (1) An AC power adapter (one end plugs into the dock connector at the bottom of your iPhone, and the other end plugs into a standard household outlet). Or (2) your iPhone will charge any time it's connected to your computer with the special USB cable (one end plugs into the dock connector, and the other end plugs into the USB input on your computer). (*Note:* There are other third-party charging solutions, like car chargers, but you have to buy those separately, so for now we're just going to focus on what comes standard with your iPhone.) Your iPhone also comes with a charging dock, which is nice because it stands your iPhone upright while it's charging (so you don't have to just lay your iPhone on a table), but other than that there's no advantage to using the Dock over just plugging your iPhone directly into your computer (whether you use the Dock or the connector cable by itself, they work the same way. The only difference is, if you use the Dock, you plug the USB cable into the dock connector on the Dock, rather than the iPhone itself).

Adjusting the Volume

There are volume controls on the top-left side of your iPhone (shown circled here in red). By default, they control the ringer volume—each time you press the top button it increases the ringer volume, and the bottom button decreases the ringer volume with each press. When you change the ringer volume using these buttons, you'll see a volume bar temporarily appear onscreen so you can easily see your current volume setting as you adjust it. Although by default these buttons control the ringer volume, these are "context sensitive controls," so once you make a call, they automatically switch to control the volume of your phone call (that way, if you're making your call in a busy place like an airport, you can turn up the volume so you can hear your call). If you're playing a song or a video using the iPod functions, the buttons switch to control their volume.

---

iTip

If you're playing music on your iPhone, and find yourself turning the volume down fairly often, it probably just means you're too old. Sorry, that was lame. (I'd like to tell you that these little comments get funnier as the book goes on, but sadly they don't.)

Using Your iPhone's Built-In Speaker

If your Apple headphones (headset) are plugged in (they're actually called "earbuds"), then you'll hear your music, videos, and even phone calls directly through them. However, your iPhone also has its own speaker and anytime your earbuds aren't plugged in, that speaker is active (it has to be—otherwise you wouldn't hear your phone ring, right?). If you want to use your iPhone's speakerphone (when you're on a phone call), just tap the Speaker button that appears onscreen while your call is in progress. When you tap that button, it will turn solid blue to let you know the speakerphone is active. To turn the speakerphone off, tap that solid blue button again.

Your iPhone's Auto-Sleep Mode

Your iPhone is very careful to conserve battery power (actually, it's pretty much obsessed with it), so if you're not actively doing something with your iPhone, in about 45 seconds it dims the brightness of the screen (to save battery power), and then about 15 seconds later, if you still haven't done anything, it thinks you're busy doing something else and it puts itself to sleep (again, to save battery power). Waking your iPhone is easy (as noted earlier): just press the Home button or tap the Sleep/Wake button at the top of your iPhone.

Mini Icon Decoder

Your iPhone displays lots of little status icons across the very top of your iPhone's touch-screen to help you know what's going on in its world. For example, the little bars on the top left show the current signal strength of your phone, followed by the name of your cell phone provider (or, if you're roaming, who you're roaming with). The next icon over shows the strength of the wireless Internet network you're connected to (if you're in an area with an open high-speed wireless network, your iPhone lets you jump on that network. If you've got a high-speed wireless connection at home or the office, it jumps on that Wi-Fi network and your email and webpages load faster than a greased pig. If not, it uses AT&T's EDGE network as your connection—you'll see a small "E" icon up top—which is somewhat slower, but not as slow as dial-up. Nothing is as slow as dial-up. Glaciers form faster than dial-up). If you see the icon of an airplane up there, you're in Airplane mode, which means your phone, email, and Internet connections are turned off (see Chapter 10 for more on Airplane mode, which you generally only use on airplanes or if you're seriously freaky about conserving battery power). If you're playing music on your iPhone, you'll see a mini Play button up there, and if you've got an alarm set (using the Clock function), then you'll see a mini clock icon. If you see a blue or white Bluetooth icon up there, it means your iPhone is connected to a Bluetooth device (like a wireless headset or Bluetooth car connection). If the Bluetooth logo is gray, Bluetooth is on, but nothing's connected. You can pretty much figure what the battery icon is for (if not, see the next page).

Finding Out How Much Battery Time Is Left

At the top-right corner of your iPhone's touchscreen is a little battery charge indicator icon. If it's solid white, you're fully charged. If it's half-filled, so is your battery. If you get low on battery power, don't worry—your iPhone will let you know. A message will appear when you're down to just a 20% battery charge, and then it will warn you again when it gets to a 10% charge. When you plug your iPhone into your computer or AC adapter to charge your iPhone, a really huge battery icon appears onscreen (it doesn't really appear—it dominates your screen), so you can see the current battery charge status from across the room.

iTip

If you're charging your iPhone, your battery charge icon (up in the top-right corner of your screen) will have a lightning bolt on it. If your battery is fully charged, it displays a power plug graphic on the battery icon instead.

Using the Built-In Keyboard

Anytime you need to type something on your iPhone, a keyboard automatically appears onscreen. If the keys look kind of small, that's only because they are. Luckily, Apple has some features that make using the keyboard a lot easier. As you type on-screen, a large version of the letter you just typed pops up in front of your fingers so you can see instantly if you hit the right letter. I can tell you from experience that the more you use this keyboard, the easier it gets, so if you wind up misspelling just about every word when you first start, don't sweat it—in just a couple of days you'll be misspelling only every third or fourth word. There's also a pretty clever auto-complete function. Although it will suggest a word while you're typing it, go ahead and finish the word (especially if you've spelled it wrong) and it will replace your misspelled word with the correct word (95% of the time). You do have to get used to typing a word, seeing that you've misspelled it, and continuing to type. If you do that—you'll be amazed at how quickly you'll be able to type using this keyboard.

---

iTip

If you need to go back and fix a typo that the auto-complete feature didn't catch, just press-and-hold approximately where the typo occured and a magnifying Loupe appears onscreen so you can not only clearly see the location of your cursor, but you can move the cursor with your finger, as well, to quickly let you fix the mistake.

Using iPhone's Touchscreen to Navigate

The touchscreen on your iPhone's high-resolution screen works amazingly well, and there are just a few little techniques to learn so you're not only very accurate when using it, but have fun as well. Here are the three biggies:

(1) Don't press too hard. It just takes a light tap on the touchscreen to activate any button or select any item.

(2) Aim your finger either at the center of the button or object you want to select, or just above the center. If you aim any lower, you'll probably select the object below what you were trying to select.

(3) To scroll on the touchscreen, or move an object (like a slider), you touch the screen lightly and just "swipe" from left to right across the screen (Apple calls this "flicking," but it feels more like a swipe to me). For example, to see the album art in your iPhone's iPod, just touch an album lightly with your finger and slide it over to the left (or right). You don't have to drag very far at all—plus, you can just kind of flick it to scroll or move faster. (Oh, now I get that whole "flicking" thing.)

Syncing Your iPhone

Syncing your iPhone just means you're connecting your iPhone to your computer (your Mac or PC) and syncing the songs, videos, contacts, calendars, etc., between the two. This happens automatically as soon as you plug in your iPhone to your computer. When your computer detects you've connected your iPhone, it launches iTunes and starts syncing your content automatically with no additional input needed from you (if you have this preference set). However, you can set preferences for exactly what gets uploaded to your iPhone. You do this in iTunes once your iPhone is connected to your computer. Simply click on your iPhone in the Devices list on the left side of the iTunes window and your iPhone preferences appear in the main iTunes window (as seen here). There are individual tabs for music, video, photos, and info (calendar, contacts, etc.). For example, click on the Music tab, and the iPhone music preferences appear, where you can choose which playlists get uploaded or if all of your playlists and songs get transferred to your iPhone.

iTip

If you add a contact to your Contacts list from right within your iPhone, the next time you sync up with your computer, it adds that contact to your computer's contact list, so both your iPhone and your computer stay "in sync." It's a "no strings attached" type of arrangement. (Did anybody get that vague *NSYNC reference? My 10-year-old did.)

Using the Apple Headset (Headphones)

SCOTT KELBY

If you're going to listen to music, or videos, or audiobooks, or…well, you get the idea, you're going to want to use the stereo headset that comes with your iPhone. It plugs right into the special headset jack at the top of the iPhone. Here's why Apple calls it a "headset" rather than "headphones": if you're listening to something on the iPhone and a call comes in, you can pause the music (or video) and take the call by pressing a tiny button attached to the headset's cord (as shown above). You don't have to pick up the phone to talk, because there's a tiny mic built into that button, which hangs on the cord right where it needs to be for you to carry on a normal conversation. (By the way, you can also use this button on the cord to switch music tracks when you're listening to your iPhone's iPod).

---

iTip

At this point, the only headphone set that fits into your iPhone is the Apple Stereo Headset that came with your iPhone. However, Belkin (www.belkin.com) sells a special iPhone headphone adapter (for around $11) that lets you plug in standard headphones (so you can use your Bose Noise Cancelling Headphones, or airline headphones, etc.). The downside is most other headphones don't come with a built-in mic attached to the cord, or a button to switch between music and an incoming call.

Using the Headset's Button

So you may be wondering, "If the button on your headset cord lets you pause the music to answer a call or skip to the next song, how does it know whether you want it to pause or skip to the next song?" Great question (wish I'd thought of it myself). To pause the music, you just click the button once. To skip to the next song, you click two times in quick succession (a double-click, if you will). But it does even more than that (this is one smart button for being so darn small). For example, if you're on one call and you get another call coming in (via call waiting), you can click once to hold the current call and jump over and take the incoming call. If you want the incoming call to go straight to your voicemail instead, then just click-and-hold the button for a few seconds and off it goes. Okay, last scenario: you're on one call and another call comes in, and you want to hang up from your first call and take this new call. You click-and-hold the button for a couple of seconds until you hear two little beeps, which lets you know that you've hung up with caller #1, and you're now on with caller #2, the winner of a call-waiting standoff.

Zooming In for a Better View

A cool feature of the touchscreen is the ability to zoom your view in tighter on webpages, emails, or in the Maps feature. You do this by either: (1) double-tapping on the area you want to zoom in to (let's say you're on a webpage and you want to zoom in to read an article. Just double-tap right on that area [it's like double-clicking with a mouse—just two quick taps], and it zooms in). Or, the second method (2) is to "pinch out," which is where you pinch your index finger and thumb together (like you're pinching something), and then you touch the screen with these two fingers pinched together and quickly spread them out. As you spread out your fingers, the screen zooms in (again, this only works on webpages, email, and the Maps feature, so if you're trying this on the All Contacts list, you're going to get really frustrated). To zoom back out, start with your fingers apart— touch the top of the screen with your index finger and the bottom with your thumb— and pinch inward until they touch (like you're trying to pinch the screen).

⌃   **iTip**

Here's a tip we all learned from our friend, author David Pogue: the secret to quickly adding any punctuation is to press-and-hold the punctuation button, and in a moment the punctuation characters will appear. Now just slide your finger over to the character you want and then remove your finger. It immediately returns you to the regular alpha-betical keyboard. Thanks for sharing that one David—we use it every single day!

Turning on Silent Mode

Stepping into a meeting? About to testify in court? Going to a meeting about your upcoming testimony in court? Then you might want to switch your iPhone to Silent mode so you're not interrupted by any errant sounds, alarms, or ringtones during the sentencing phase of your trial. You do this by moving the Ring/Silent switch (found on the top-left side of your iPhone, and circled here in red) to the Silent mode (which has you moving the switch toward the back of the iPhone. Don't worry—you'll see a large icon appear onscreen to indicate which mode you've just switched to). If your case is dismissed, you can switch back to regular Ring mode by moving the Ring/Silent switch back towards the screen side of your iPhone.

When the iPhone Rings...

When you hear your iPhone ring, that's a pretty good indication that someone's calling you (I'm sorry—I just couldn't resist). When you do get a call, your iPhone displays the number of the person who's calling (or it displays their name if they're already in your All Contacts list). Now, if your iPhone is sleeping (it's been in your pocket, or your purse, etc.), you can answer the call by dragging the green Slide to Answer button to the right. To ignore the call (and have it go straight to your voicemail), just press the Sleep/Wake button (once) at the top of the iPhone, which also silences the ring. If a call comes in while your iPhone is wide awake (for example, you're not on the phone, but you're using another part of the iPhone, like checking your email or checking out a website), then two buttons will appear at the bottom of the screen: To accept the call, press the green Answer button. To decline the call (and send it straight into your voicemail), press the red Decline button (doing this also immediately silences the ring).

iTip

If for whatever reason you don't pass the AT&T credit check requirements, rumor has it that AT&T does offer an alternative pay-as-you-go plan for the iPhone. In the activation process, you'll be offered the ability to pay a deposit, which means going in person to the AT&T store. You'll then be offered a GoPhone plan.

iPhone Accessories & Third-Party Applications

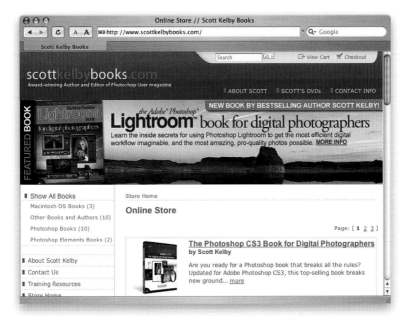

There are new accessories coming out daily for the iPhone. Our favorites to date are the Belkin Headphone Adapter for iPhone, which allows you to connect your regular earbuds or headphones to the iPhone's recessed audio jack, and the Griffin Technology PowerJolt for iPhone, which allows you to charge your iPhone in your car (other adapters work, too). However, since there will be so many accessories that come out after this book goes to press, we thought we'd give you a bonus by being able to check out our favorite accessories for the iPhone online anytime. Check http://www.scottkelby.com/iphonegear or http://terrywhite.com/techblog for the latest iPhone accessory reviews.

Chapter Two
Phoneheads
How to Use the iPhone's Phone

 I thought "Phoneheads" was a great name for this chapter, but it's not the name of a song; it's the name of a band that plays electronic music, which is why you probably haven't heard of them. My guess is that you don't listen to much electronic music. I'm not talking about music made with electronics (like electric guitars or synths), I'm talking about the kind of music you hear your teenagers playing, and you shake your head in disgust telling them, "That's not music!" Then one day, when you hear Van Halen's "Jamie's Cryin'" playing on your oldies station, you look in your rear view mirror and tell your kids, "Now that's music!" The sad thing is—you're right. That was music. And the stuff kids are listening to today is nothing more than an aural assault on everything we hold sacred about "real" music which includes: white headbands, skinny ties, parachute pants, big hair, the hood of Whitesnake's car, inexpensive gas, and cassette tapes. Now *that* was music. I'm pretty safe in saying all this because you bought an iPhone, which means you must be pretty well off (or just incredibly loose with money), because iPhones aren't cheap. That means you're probably in your late 30s or early 40s, and you think that electronic music isn't music, so when I wrote that earlier, you were nodding your head. But, there is a second scenario: one in which you're young, and have rich parents, and they bought you an iPhone because they're loose with money. In that case, make sure you check out Phonehead's track "Syrinx (TGM Mix)." I love that song!

23

Importing Contacts from Your Computer

If you're a Macintosh user, there are three applications that let you sync directly from your computer to your iPhone, and they are: (1) your Mac's Address Book application (shown above), (2) Microsoft Entourage (see Chapter 9 for how to set this up), or (3) Yahoo! Address Book. If your contacts are in any of those three, when you plug your iPhone into your computer, it launches iTunes and syncs the contacts on your computer with your iPhone (if you have this preference set). Pretty simple stuff.

If you're a Windows user, it works pretty much the same way, but the three contact managers it supports direct importing from are: (1) Yahoo! Address Book, (2) Windows Address Book, and (3) Microsoft Outlook.

Importing Contacts from Your Old Phone

Okay, this gets a little stickier (well, at least stickier than what we did on the previous page, which was import contacts already on your computer in a contact manager). So, here's the thing: what you have to do is (you knew this was coming, right?) get the contacts in your old phone onto your computer. Then you can go back to the previous page and follow those instructions. On the Mac, there's a utility program called iSync (made by Apple and already installed on every Macintosh made in the past few years) that does the syncing from your phone to your computer for you, and it imports your contact info into Apple's own Address Book application (which syncs with your iPhone, no sweat). If you're on a Windows PC, you can use a utility called DataPilot, which syncs your current "old-fashioned" phone (it supports over 650 models of phones, including phones from Nokia, Motorola, Samsung, LG, and Erikson, among others) with your computer (do a Google search and you'll find it in all of five seconds). Again, once you get your contacts on your computer, then follow the instructions on the previous page.

Dialing Using the Standard Keypad

If you want to dial a number, you can just type in the number (like you would on any other phone) by tapping once on the Phone button, then tapping on the Keypad button to bring up the standard phone dialing buttons you see above. To dial a number, just tap the number keys. If you make a mistake, press the Back button (the button to the right of the green Call button) to erase that digit.

iTip

If you're on the iPhone and in an area that gets pretty weak reception, you might try moving your hand away from the black plastic cover that appears on the back of the iPhone, near the bottom. That's where the internal antenna is located, and moving your hand away from that part of the iPhone might help the signal strength. Hey, it couldn't hurt.

Saving a Dialed Number as a Contact

If you've just entered a number using the keypad, and you realize you'd like to add it as a contact (so you can dial it again in the future with just one tap), then once the full number appears at the top of the Keypad screen (as seen here), tap the Add Contact button (which appears to the immediate left of the green Call button). This brings up a dialog asking if you want to save this as a new contact, or if you want to add this number to an existing contact.

Manually Adding Contacts

If you want to add a contact manually (by manually, I mean just typing it right into your iPhone), just tap on the Phone button, then on the Contacts button, then tap the + (plus sign) button in the upper right-hand corner. This brings up a New Contact screen, and to add some contact info, just tap on the info you want to add (for example, to add your new contact's email address, just tap on Add New Email and a screen appears ready for you to type in their email address on the keyboard at the bottom of the screen). When you're done entering the email address, tap the Save button in the top-right corner of that screen, and you return to the New Contact screen to add more info the same way.

---

iTip

Here's a tip to help you think like your iPhone. Most of the time, if you see a button in the upper-left corner of the screen, it acts like a Back button in a Web browser—pressing it will take you back to the previous screen you were on.

Dialing Someone in Your Contacts List

To dial someone in your Contacts list, tap on the Phone button, then tap on the Contacts button (okay, that was pretty obvious), and then tap on the person's name in the list. This brings up their full contact info including a list of all their phone numbers you have added (cell number, home, office, etc.). To dial one of those numbers, just tap once on it and it starts dialing.

 iTip

When you're in the All Contacts list, if you want to jump directly to a particular letter quickly, just tap once on the letter in the alphabetic list on the far-right side of the screen. You can also tap, hold, and slide up/down the list, as well.

Seeing Each Contact's Photo When They Call

How would you like for each contact's photo to appear when they call you? (It's great for seeing who's calling at just a glance—without having to read their name or figure out who it is.) There are two ways to do this: (1) use a photo already on your iPhone, or (2) take a photo using the iPhone's built-in camera and use that photo. Start at the Home screen, then tap the Phone button, then the Contacts button. Scroll to the contact you want to assign a photo to, then tap the Edit button in the top-right corner of the screen. When the Info screen appears, in the upper-left corner, tap on Add Photo. This brings up two new buttons: Take Photo (so you can take a photo of your contact using the iPhone's built-in camera), and Choose Existing Photo (which lets you choose any photo you've already imported into your iPhone). Tap whichever one you want. If you tapped the Choose Existing Photo button, it takes you to your Photo Albums screen where you can tap on the photo you want to assign to your contact. This brings you to a screen where you can determine the size and position of the photo that will display when your contact calls (use your finger to slide it around, which basically crops the photo, or "pinch it" with your fingers to scale it up or down). When it looks good to you, tap the gray Set Photo button and you're done. If instead you tapped the Take Photo button, just take the photo, scale and move it, and tap Set Photo. This is cool, but the picture won't be in the Camera Roll for download later. So if it's a picture you will want to use for other purposes, take the picture first and add it to the contact afterwards.

Shooting a Photo and Adding It to a Contact

Start at the Home screen, then tap on the Camera button. Aim the camera and take a photo of your contact by tapping the camera shutter button at the bottom center of the screen. You'll hear the shutter sound to let you know the photo has been taken, but to see the photo you just took, you have to tap the stacked photos button that appears to the left of the camera shutter button. This brings up the Camera Roll screen, where you'll see little thumbnails of the photos you've taken. Tap the photo you want to assign, and it will appear full screen. Now, a row of buttons appears along the bottom of the screen. Tap the button on the far left and a pop-up menu will appear onscreen. To assign this photo to a contact, tap the Assign To Contact button, and it brings up your All Contacts list. Tap on the contact you want to assign that photo to, and it shows you a preview of how the final photo is going to look when the contact calls, so you can move and scale it the way you want (using your finger to slide the photo around onscreen, which basically crops the photo to your liking, or "pinching it" with your fingers to scale it up or down). When it looks good to you, press the gray Set Photo button and you're done.

Turn a Recent Caller into a Contact

If someone has just called you that isn't in your All Contacts list (but you'd like to add them as a contact), start at the Home screen, tap on the Phone button, then tap on Recents. Scroll to the number of the person you want to add as a contact, then tap on the button with the arrow in the blue circle to the right of their number. This brings up an info screen and at the bottom of this screen you'll see a button called Create New Contact. Tap that button and the New Contact screen appears with their phone number already entered for you—you just have to type in their name, address, etc. When you're done, tap the Save button in the upper-right corner of the screen.

iTip

If you'd like to add a note to a contact (like a description of who this person is, or how you know them), tap on the contact, and when their Info screen appears, tap on the Edit button (in the top-right corner). Then in the Info edit screen that appears, scroll down and tap on Add Field, then scroll down and tap on Note to add a Note field. This brings up the Edit Note field where you can type in your note using the keyboard that appears at the bottom of the screen.

Assigning Ringtones to Specific Callers

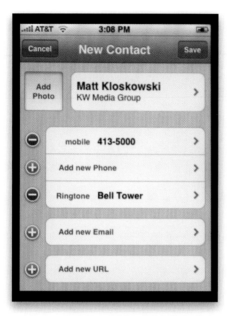

If you'd like to assign a ringtone to a specific caller (for example, I have a ringtone as-signed to my wife's cell phone number, so I instantly know it's her without even looking at my phone), here's what to do: Start at the Home screen, then tap the green Phone button, then tap the Contacts button. Tap on the contact you want to assign a ringtone to, then when their Info screen appears, tap the blue Edit button in the top-right corner of the screen. When the edit Info screen appears, tap on Assign Ringtone. This brings you to the Ringtones screen, with a list of all your ringtones. To assign a ringtone to this contact, just tap on one (it will play a sample of the ringtone when you tap on it). When you find the ringtone you want, just tap the blue Info button at the top left of the screen, and it returns you to the edit Info screen where you can tap the blue Done button in the top-right corner of the screen to lock in the ringtone change. Now when this contact calls, you'll hear their custom ringtone rather than the default ringtone that you'll hear when anyone else calls.

 iTip

The iPhone can sync notes from your calendar entries and contacts. So if you have notes in another application that you want to sync from your computer, add them to your contacts or calendar entries to get them on the iPhone.

The iPhone's Version of Speed Dial

iPhone's name for speed dial is "Favorites," and to turn one of your contacts into a Favorite, just tap on the name in your All Contacts list to view the screen with their full contact info. Then, in the bottom-right corner of their Info screen, tap on the Add to Favorites button (as shown here), and that contact is added to your Favorites screen. Now, there is another way to do it, and that is to start at the Favorites screen (you tap the Favorites button), then tap the little + (plus sign) button in the upper-right corner of the Favorites screen. This brings up your All Contacts list, and you just tap on the name of the contact you want added to your Favorites. If your contact has only one phone number (like just a home number, or just a cell number), they're immediately added as a Favorite. If they have multiple numbers, then it brings up all their numbers and you just tap on the number you want added as a Favorite.

Removing a Favorite

If you decide that someone's not your Favorite anymore (hey, it happens), you can easily remove them. Just tap the Edit button in the top-left corner of the Favorites screen, then a red circle with a – (minus sign) will appear before each Favorite. To remove a Favorite from your list, just tap directly on its red minus button, and a red Remove button will appear to its right (as seen above). Tap that Remove button and it's gone!

Reordering Your Favorites

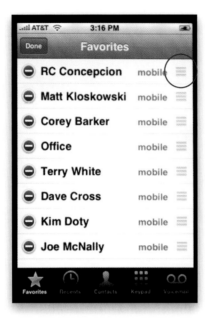

If you don't like the order you added your Favorites in, you can reorder them. Just tap on the Edit button, and then on the far right of each contact, just past the type of phone number (mobile, home, etc.), you'll see three short horizontal lines (circled in red above). Now, you're going to drag your contacts into the order you want them by tapping-and-holding on those lines and dragging your contact up (or down) until they're in the order you want them (it's easier than it sounds).

Seeing the Contact Info for a Favorite

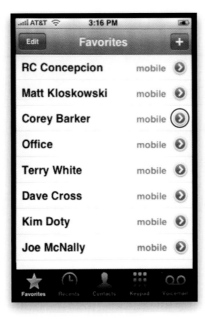

To see the full contact info for any of your Favorites, just tap once on the little blue circle with a right-facing arrow that appears to the right of the contact (shown circled above), and the full Info screen appears for that contact.

The Advantage of Contact Groups

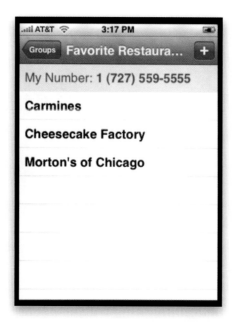

If the contact manager on your computer allows you to have caller groups, this can make getting to the contacts you want much easier. For example, you could have a group for your favorite restaurants, and one just for your friends, and one for your co-workers, and...well, you get the idea. That way, when you go to the All Contacts screen, you can tap the Groups button (in the upper-left corner) to see a list of your different groups. Then, you can tap on a group and see just those contacts (like seeing just your favorite restaurants, as shown above).

How to Know If You Missed Any Calls

If you miss a call, you'll see the caller's name and Missed Call onscreen when you wake your iPhone from sleep (well, you'll see their name if they're in your Contacts list. If they're not, you'll just see their number and Missed Call). If you missed a call, when you press the Home button, you'll see the green Phone button now has a small red circle on its top-right corner with the number of calls you missed. Okay, here's where it gets a little weird: that number is not actually the number of calls you've missed, it's the calls you've missed combined with the number of unheard phone messages you've been left. So, if you missed five calls but those five callers all left messages, then you'll see the number 10, which represents those five missed calls and five voicemail messages, even though only five people actually called. I told you it was weird.

Returning Missed Calls

To return a missed call, on the Home screen, tap the green Phone button, then tap the Recents button at the bottom of the screen. This brings up a list of all recent calls, and the calls you see listed in red are your missed calls. To return a missed call, just tap on it and it dials that number. (*Note:* The number of missed calls appears in a small red circle in the top-right corner of the Recents button.)

iTip

To clear any missed calls and your list of recent calls, go to the Recents screen and tap the Clear button in the top-right corner of the screen.

Seeing If You Have Messages

If a caller left you a voicemail message, you'll see the caller's name (if they're in your Contacts list—if not, their phone number) when you wake your iPhone from sleep. When you tap the green Phone button, you'll see the Voicemail button, and on it you'll see a red circle displaying the number of messages you have waiting. To see a list of your voicemails (yes, you see a list—that's why Apple calls this "Visual Voicemail"), tap on the Voicemail button, and you'll see a list of the contacts (or numbers) who've left you a voicemail message, and when they called (as seen above). Messages with a round blue button before them haven't been listened to yet.

Deleting Heard Voicemails

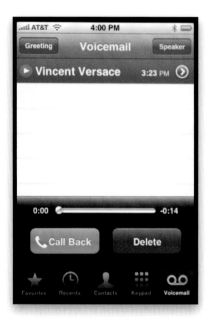

The beauty of this system is you don't have to listen to your messages in order—you can tap directly on the message you want to hear and that message plays (you'll have to hold the iPhone up to your ear to hear the message). To hear your messages through your iPhone's speaker, tap the Speaker button on the top right. You'll see a status bar that moves from left to right as your message plays, which gives you a visual cue as to how long the message actually is. Now, here's the thing: when a message is new, you just tap on it and it plays. But once you've heard it once, the rules change—now to hear a voicemail, you tap on the message you want to hear, and a little blue Play/Pause button appears before that message. To hear the message again, tap that little blue button. To pause the message, tap that same little blue button again. To return a call, tap on the message, then tap the green Call Back button. To delete a message, tap on it, then tap on the red Delete button. Once you delete a message, it's not really deleted from your iPhone—it just moves that message to a deleted area (kind of the way deleting a file on your computer just puts it in your Trash or Recycle Bin). You can still see, and hear, your deleted messages by tapping on (I know—it's pretty obvious) Deleted Messages (at the end of your voicemail list). Once there, to move a deleted message back to your regular list, just tap on it, then tap the gray Undelete button. However, if you really want this voicemail off your iPhone for good, tap on the message and tap the Clear All button.

Replay Just Part of a Message

This is an iPhone feature I just love: while your message is playing, you can grab the little slider and "scrub" back a few seconds and hear anything you just missed—in real time. So, for example, let's say you're listening to a message and the person on the message gives you a phone number. To hear that phone number again (without having to listen to the entire message again), you can just tap-and-hold on the little status bar knob and drag it back a little bit (just like you would scrub through a video), and hear it again. Yes, other phones can do something similar, but because you're dragging the audio live, you can quickly drag right to the spot you want to hear again. Try it once, and you'll see the difference it makes.

Putting a Call on Hold to Call Someone Else

If you're on a call and need to make another call, you can put that call on hold and make a different call (kind of like having a two-line phone). Just tap the Hold button on the touchscreen, then tap the Add Call button. This brings up your All Contacts list, and you can tap on a name to dial that contact, or you can just dial a number by tapping on the Keypad button that appears in the bottom-right corner of the All Contacts screen. If you want to switch back to your original call, you can just tap the Swap button.

iTip

When you have two calls going at the same time (one live and one on hold), you can see which call is currently "live" by looking at your phone's screen, and you'll see both calls listed at the top of the screen. The one with the little phone icon beside it is the live call.

Recording Your Outgoing Message

By default, you get a generic "I'm not here, man" voicemail message, but creating your own custom message is just too easy to continue using that default message. Just tap on the Voicemail button, then in the top-right corner of the Voicemail screen, tap on the Greeting button to bring up the Greeting screen. You'll see two choices: (a) Default (the generic pre-recorded greeting), and (b) Custom (where you create your own). Tap on Custom, and Play and Record buttons appear at the bottom of the screen. Tap the white Record button, hold the iPhone up to your ear (like you are answering a call), and just say your message into it. When you're done, tap the red Stop button, and to hear it, tap the blue Play button. If you don't like your message, just tap the white Record button again and record a new message. When it sounds good to you, tap the Save button in the upper-right corner of the screen.

iTip

Don't sing messages into your iPhone, as a sensor was designed by Apple to detect really bad singing and when it analyzes your voice and determines that it is indeed bad singing, it automatically forwards your message, along with a picture of you, to YouTube where it's then featured in a public humiliation forum. Well, at least that's what I've been told.

Sending Text Messages

There are two ways to send text messages from your iPhone: From the Home screen, (1) tap directly on the green SMS Text button (upper-left corner), which brings up the Text Messages screen. In the upper-right corner, there's a button that is a square icon with a pen in it—tap on that button and the New Message screen appears, where you enter your contact's name (or phone number if they're not in your Contacts list), and then type in your message using the keyboard (if you want to choose a contact from your Contacts list, just tap on the + [plus sign] button to the right of the To field and your All Contacts list will appear). Or (2) you can tap the Phone button, tap on the Contacts button, and tap on any contact. Once their contact info appears, tap the Text Message button (it's below all their contact info). This brings up the same New Message screen, where you compose your text message. When you're done entering your message, just tap the Send button and your message is sent.

Reading Text Messages

If you've received a text message, you'll see the name of the person who sent it (if they're in your Contacts list) and the first two lines of their message as soon as you wake the iPhone from sleep. When you go to the Home screen, you'll now see a little red circle added to the top right of the green SMS Text button with the number of unread text messages you have waiting. Tap on that SMS Text button and you'll see your new message. To see a list of all your text messages, tap on the Messages button in the upper-left corner. To see any message in the list, just tap on it. Now it gets fun: if you are texting back and forth, you'll see your text conversation appear in "talk bubbles" (as seen above). Your messages appear in a green bubble, replies appear in a gray bubble, and visually it looks like you're having a conversation (if you're a Macintosh user, you'll probably recognize this, as it looks just like Apple's iChat online chat software that comes on all Macs).

---

iTip

When you're typing a message, don't sweat little misspellings as iPhone will normally catch them and fix them for you. Just keep typing and watch how it "cleans up after you" and fixes the spelling of the words. It takes a little getting used to—typing and letting the typos stand—but give it a try and you'll be amazed at how well it works.

Muting Your Call/Hearing Through Speaker

If you're on a call and don't want the caller to hear what you're saying for a moment, tap the Mute button on the touchscreen. When you're ready to start talking again, tap the Mute button again. If you have a call in progress and want to hear your conversation through the iPhone's speaker, tap the Speaker button on the touchscreen.

Making Instant Conference Calls

This is another one of those features that will make you fall in love with your iPhone. To add another person to your call in progress (for a three-way call), just tap the Add Call button on the touchscreen, and it brings up your All Contacts screen. Tap the contact's name you want added to your three-way call, and it not only dials them, but adds them to your existing conversation. If the person you want added to your call isn't in your All Contacts list, then you can dial them by tapping once on the Keypad button in the bottom-right corner of the All Contacts screen.

Dialing an Extension

I know—how hard could it be? Actually, it's easy—if you know how. So, let's say you dial a number and you get one of those "If you know your party's extension, please dial it now" greetings. All you have to do is tap the Keypad button on your touchscreen, and then dial the extension. I know, it sounds really easy now, but I've seen people totally stumped when it happens to them.

Check Your Email While You're On the Phone

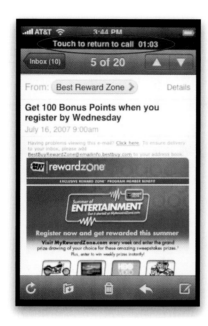

If you're in a really boring phone conversation, do what everybody else in the business world does—check your email. It makes things easier if you start by tapping the Speaker button (so you can still hear your conversation while you're looking at the touchscreen). Then press the Home button, then tap the Mail button. Don't worry—your call will stay live even though you're doing something completely different. However, there's always a chance that the person you're talking with will also become bored, and start checking their email. It's a chance you have to take. Anyway, to return to your call screen, just tap once at the very top of your screen (where it says Touch to Return to Call), and it takes you back there.

Pausing the Music to Take a Call

If you've got your headset (earbuds) on and you're listening to music and a phone call comes in, you can pause the song and jump over to take the call all in one click (that's right—it's a click, not a tap). There's a little tiny button attached to the earbuds (about 10" from the right earbud itself. It doesn't look like a button, it looks like a thin little plastic rectangle). Click that button, and the song playing is paused, and it answers your call. When you're done with the call, click the button again to hang up and pick up the song right where you left off.

Ignoring an Incoming Call

If a call comes in, and you can't take the call right then, but don't want the phone to continue ringing, then just press the Sleep/Wake button on the top of the iPhone. This stops the ringing and sends the call into your voicemail.

Turning the Ringer Off

If you don't want to hear your iPhone's ringer at all, press the Home button, then tap on the Settings button. When the Settings screen shows up, tap on Sounds, then in the Ring section, tap-and-drag the Ring volume slider (it's directly below the Vibrate setting) all the way to the left. This turns your ring volume off. By default, your phone will still vibrate when a call comes in, but there won't be an audible ring. If you want to turn that vibration off as well, in the Ring section, switch the Vibrate control to the OFF setting by tapping once just to the right of the blue ON setting.

Choosing Your Ringtone

The default ringtone for your iPhone is a marimba sound, but if you'd like to change it, start at the Home screen, then tap on the Settings button. When the Settings screen appears, tap on Sounds, then under the Ring volume slider you'll see the Ringtone control. Tap on Ringtone and it takes you to a screen listing all the built-in ringtones (currently, you can't assign a song in your iPod application as a ringtone). You'll see a checkmark appear to the right of Marimba indicating that it's the currently selected ringtone. To change ringtones, tap on the name of the ringtone you want. That ring-tone plays (so you can hear if you really want to select it), and if you want to keep this new sound as your ringtone, just leave that screen (tap the Sounds button in the top-left corner of the Ringtone screen, or press the Home button).

Stop People You Call from Seeing Your Number

If you want to call somebody, but you'd prefer that they not see your iPhone's number, you can turn off the feature that shares your number with whomever you call. To do that, start at the Home screen, then tap on the Settings button. When the Settings screen appears, scroll down and tap on Phone. When the Phone settings screen appears, scroll down and you'll find a control called Show My Caller ID. To keep your number private, tap on that control and it brings up the Show My Caller ID screen with an ON/OFF button. Now tap to the immediate right of the blue ON setting to switch this feature off.

Setting Up Call Forwarding

To have calls coming into your iPhone forwarded to another phone, start at the Home screen, then tap on the Settings button. When the Settings screen appears, scroll down and tap on Phone. When the Phone settings screen appears, scroll down to Call Forwarding. Tap on Call Forwarding to bring up the Call Forwarding screen. You'll see an ON/OFF button (and by default, Call Forwarding is set to OFF). To turn it on, tap once to the immediate left of the OFF setting to turn Call Forwarding on. Now, you're probably wondering where your call is forwarded to. Once you turn on the Call Forwarding feature, if you don't already have a Forwarding To number entered, a screen where you enter the phone number to forward to will appear. Now, this next part throws a lot of people: there's no "OK" or "Save" button. You just have to tap the Call Forwarding button in the top-left corner and it returns you to the main Call Forwarding screen, where you'll see the number you just added and the ON setting. When you want to turn the Call Forwarding feature off, go back to the same screen (follow the steps above), and tap the ON setting and it will change to the OFF setting.

Using Apple's Bluetooth Wireless Headset

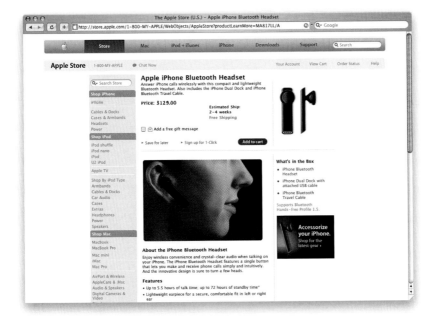

You can use the "hands-free" feature of your iPhone if you've bought either Apple's iPhone Bluetooth Headset, a third-party Bluetooth wireless headset, or if your car supports hands-free talking using your car's built-in Bluetooth feature, so your conversation happens through your car's stereo speakers and built-in mic (this feature is becoming more and more common in new cars). If you bought Apple's wireless Bluetooth headset, the setup is a breeze because it comes with a charging/syncing Dual Dock that holds your iPhone and your Apple wireless headset. You just plug the Dual Dock into your computer (or into a power outlet using the included charger), then put both your iPhone and your wireless headset in the Dual Dock, and it automatically syncs (called "autopairing") your iPhone to your wireless headset.

Other Headsets or Bluetooth in Your Car

If you have a third-party Bluetooth wireless headset, or you want to pair your iPhone to your car's Bluetooth feature, here's what to do: First you have to put your headset (or your car's Bluetooth feature) in "Discoverable" mode, which means you put it in a mode where other Bluetooth devices can find it. How this is done is different for every headset or car make and model, so look at your headset's instruction manual (or your car's owner's manual) for how to make it "discoverable". Once it's discoverable, start at the Home screen, then tap on the Settings button. In the Settings screen, tap on General, then tap on Bluetooth. When the Bluetooth screen appears, tap to the immediate left of OFF to turn your iPhone's Bluetooth feature on. This starts your iPhone searching for any discoverable Bluetooth devices (like your wireless headset or your car's Bluetooth feature) that are within about 30 feet of where you are. Once it finds a Bluetooth device, it displays that device's name. Tap on the name, and in the next screen, enter the device's PIN (check the instructions that come with your headset or car kit for how to find this information). Tap the Connect button and they are paired (luckily, you only have to go through this process the first time. After that, it automatically recognizes your headset, or car).

Chapter Three
Please Mr. Postman
Getting (and Sending) Email on Your iPhone

 This is an incredibly important chapter, because email is incredibly important. If it weren't for the iPhone's ability to get email, I would have missed an amazing adventure. It all started with a desperate email from a Mr. Mabutuu, who (according to the email) had been a high-ranking government official in the small African nation of Nantango. I soon learned of the overthrow of his small, friendly government through a military coup that nearly cost him his life. He was able to flee to the safety of a small village protected by freedom fighters loyal to his ousted government, but before he fled the capital, he was able to move nearly $16 million of his government's surplus cash (in U.S. funds) to a small bank in a neighboring country. His main concern was that these funds not fall into the hands of the corrupt general who led the rebellion against him, and he asked if I would be so kind as to help him find a suitable U.S. bank where he could wire the $16 million. For my small role in providing my bank account number, username, password, and social security number, he would gladly share the $16 million with me rather than see it seized by the new hostile government (he proposed a 60/40 split, but I was able to negotiate it to 50/50). However, he was in a bind because before his bank would transfer the funds to my bank account, he would have to first pay $22,800 for the required doc stamps and tariffs to complete the wire transfer. Of course, I immediately wired the $22,800 to his overseas account, and since then, each day I patiently check my account for the transfer of the $16 million to hit (that's going to be a pretty exciting day for us both, eh?).

Setting Up Your Email (POP, IMAP, or Yahoo)

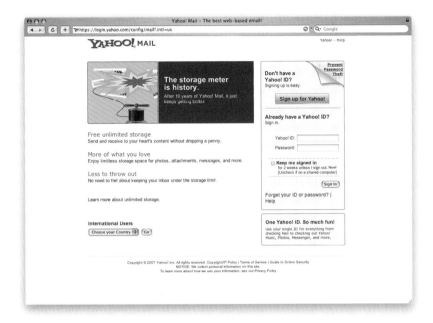

The iPhone supports the most common email standards. Luckily, if your email is already set up on your computer, then you'll have the option in iTunes to choose which email accounts you want to have working on your iPhone. If you don't have an email account yet or prefer not to use your existing email accounts, you can set up a free one on services like Yahoo.com, Google.com, and AOL.com. If you can't decide, I highly recommend using a free account on Yahoo.com. Why? Because setting up an account at www.mail .yahoo.com will give you a free "push" type email for your iPhone. This means that instead of having to check for new messages, the emails will come to the phone automatically. All other types of accounts will need to be checked, which the iPhone can do automatically at regular intervals. The iPhone also has Microsoft Exchange IMAP support, but your company's IT department has to enable this feature on the server first.

iTip

If you have a choice between POP- or IMAP-based email, choose IMAP. The reason is that IMAP email resides on a server. When you read an email on your iPhone, it will be marked as read on the server so that when you go to your computer to check email, you won't have to read the ones you've already read. Same goes for trashing an email. Once trashed on the iPhone, it will be trashed on your computer, too.

Add an Email Account Right on the iPhone

If you choose not to have your email accounts brought over from your computer, you can add them directly on the iPhone. To do this you'll need to know some things first. You'll need to know your:

- email address: you@somewhere.com
- email server type: POP, IMAP, or Exchange
- incoming server address (a.k.a. POP server): mail.domain.com
- outgoing server address (a.k.a. SMTP server): smtp.domain.com

Also, most outgoing mail servers require some kind of authentication for sending mail out when you're not on their network. You'll need to check with your ISP to find out what settings to use. Most ISPs display this info in the help section of their websites. When you set up your account, you probably received an email with all of this info.

Once you have this info, tap the Settings button on the iPhone and go to Mail, then under Accounts, tap Add Account. What's nice is that if your email account is on Yahoo, Google (Gmail), .Mac, or AOL, the iPhone will know most of the geeky settings. All you'll need is your account info. If your account is not on one of these services, then tap Other and you'll have to key in the info that you gathered above.

Checking Your Email

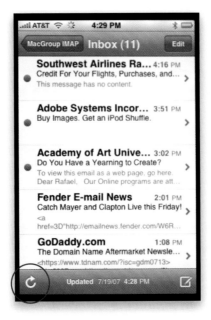

The iPhone is pretty smart in that there really isn't a check email button. It assumes that when you tap the Mail button, you probably want to check your email. At that time it checks for new messages provided you have either a Wi-Fi connection or connection to AT&T's EDGE data network. Just tap the Mail button on the Home screen and the iPhone will check for new messages. Once you're looking at your Inbox, you can also have the iPhone check for new mail immediately by tapping the curved arrow icon in the lower-left corner of the screen.

iTip

You can change your settings for Mail to automatically check for new messages every 15 minutes, every 30 minutes, or every hour. The more often the iPhone checks for email, the more it will use the battery. I chose every 30 minutes as a happy medium.

Reading Your Email

Once your email is set up and the messages start rolling in, they will be listed under the account that you set up. Unread messages will have a blue dot to the left of them. By default, the iPhone displays the first two lines of each message. You can then decide which emails you want to read in what order. When you want to display the entire email, just tap on the one you want to read and the email body will be displayed. You can scroll down the message by flicking your finger up on the screen. It's kind of counterintuitive at first because it's the opposite of the way you do it on your computer. Just think of flicking as the way you want the message to move. You want it to move up, so that you can read more of what's below. If the type is too small, you can use the pinch feature to zoom in and out: using two fingers on the display, such as your index finger and thumb, you spread them out to zoom in on the message, then pinch them in to zoom back out. You can also pan around the message by simply moving your finger around on the display in the direction you want the message to move. You can use the up and down arrows in the upper-right corner to navigate to the next message or previous message.

 iTip

You can mark a message that you are reading as unread by tapping the Details button in the upper-right corner of the message, then you will see a blue dot with Mark as Unread. Just tap this button and the message will stay marked as new.

Viewing Email Attachments

The iPhone supports viewing attachments such as JPG, PDF, Microsoft Word, and Microsoft Excel files. If you receive an image such as a JPG, Mail does a great job showing the image right in the body of the message. If you receive one of the other file types in an email on your iPhone, the attachment will generally be at the bottom of the email message. Simply tap the attachment to view it. The iPhone will slide the message over to the left and show you the attachment in a separate screen. Once you're done viewing it, you can tap the Message button at the top of the screen to go back to the original email. If you have more than one attachment, you can view the next one once you return to the message.

iTip

The fastest way to delete an email (after you've read it, or if it's obviously SPAM, even before you read it) is to just swipe left to right over the time the email came in. This reveals a red Delete button, and to delete that email just tap on the button.

Dialing a Phone Number from an Email

You have to remember that the iPhone is a phone. Therefore, if someone sends you an email that contains a phone number, you can simply tap the phone number to dial it. The iPhone will automatically switch over to the Phone application and place the call. Once you're finished with your call, you can tap the End Call button. This will take you back to your email message.

iTip

The iPhone currently doesn't have a way to copy-and-paste a phone number from one application to the next. However, if you want to add a phone number to an existing contact or create a new contact with that phone number, tap the phone number you received in an email (or on a webpage in Safari) to dial it. Then tap End Call immediately. Now the call will show up in your Recents call list in the Phone application. From there, you can tap the right arrow to the right of the phone number and have the option to either Create New Contact or Add to Existing Contact.

Going to a Website from an Email Message

The iPhone does a great job of receiving HTML-style emails. The links in your email message, whether they are text links or links on images, are live. So tapping a link in an email will automatically fire up Safari (the Web browser application) and take you to the site that you tapped on in your email message. Once you're done browsing the site, you'll have to press the Home button and then tap the Mail button again to return to the message you were viewing.

---

iTip

Once you're in Safari and looking at the page you went to from the email message, you can bookmark it by tapping the + (plus sign) to the left of the URL. Once you add this bookmark, it will be automatically synced back to your computer the next time you sync your iPhone.

Replying to an Email Message

When you want to reply to a message, tap the arrow pointing to the left in the toolbar at the bottom of the email message (the second button from the right) and you will be presented with a pop-up menu. You will have a choice of Reply (Reply All if the message was sent to more than one person) or Forward. When you tap Reply, you'll be presented with a new message already addressed to the original sender and with the original subject. The cursor will already be in the body and all you have to do is start typing your reply. If the original message was sent to you and other people, you can tap the Reply All button to send your reply to the original sender and all the people that the message was sent or copied to. Once you've typed your reply, simply hit the Send button in the upper-right corner. If you tap the Cancel button, you'll be prompted with the option to Save or Don't Save the message.

Filing an Email Message in a Folder

If you have an IMAP-based email account, it is possible to have additional folders on the server to store your messages in. You can move your iPhone email into any of these folders, as well. Since IMAP account folders reside on a server, the next time you check email on your computer or the webmail interface that your ISP provided, the mail you moved using your iPhone will be in the folder you moved it to. To move a message to a folder, bring up the message from your Inbox and tap the Move button on the bottom toolbar. Its icon looks like an arrow pointing down over a folder. You will then be presented with a list of folders to move the message to. Tap the folder you want to move it to and your iPhone will move it. If you have a POP-based email account, you can still use this feature to move a message to the Drafts, Sent, or Trash folders. However, these folders only exist on your iPhone and the message will not be in these folders on your computer.

Deleting an Email Message

Once you've read a message and you decide that you don't need to keep it any longer, you can move the message to the Trash folder. While the message is displayed, you can tap the Trash button on the bottom toolbar to move the message to the Trash. For IMAP-based accounts, the message will be in the Trash when you get back to your computer. Let's say you get a message that you know you want to delete without even reading it. You can do this right from the Inbox. Simply flick your finger across the message in the Inbox and a Delete button will appear. Tap the Delete button to delete the message. Lastly, you can also delete messages from the Inbox by tapping the Edit button at the top right of the Inbox. A red circle will appear next to each message and you can tap the circle of the message you want to delete to get the Delete button and delete it.

Forwarding an Email

Sometimes you might want to forward a message that you've received to other contacts. To forward a message that you're viewing, tap the left-pointing arrow at the bottom of the screen. You will get a pop-up menu that offers a choice between Reply, Forward, and Cancel. Tap Forward and the message will come up with the cursor in the To field. You can then either key in the name of the contact that you want to forward it to, or the email address that you want to forward it to. If you start typing a name that is already one of your saved contacts, the iPhone will present you with a list of contacts to choose from. The more letters you type, the more it will narrow down the list. If you just want to choose a contact directly, you can tap the + (plus sign) button to the right of the To field to choose one of your contacts. After putting in your first contact, if you want to forward this message to additional contacts, just start typing in a new name and the list will pop up again for you to choose the contact that you want to forward this message to. You can also carbon copy (CC) additional contacts.

Composing a New Email Message

Being able to email on the go is one of the best features of the iPhone. To create a new email message from scratch, you must first go to the Mail application from the Home screen. Once you're there, you can tap the Compose button at the bottom right of the screen from your Mailboxes screen, Inbox (or other mailbox), or while you're viewing any email message. A blank email message will appear with the cursor in the To field. You can then either key in the name of the contact that you want to send it to, or the email address that you want to send it to. If you start typing a name that is already one of your saved contacts, the iPhone will present you with a list of contacts to choose from. The more letters you type, the more it will narrow down the list. If you just want to choose a contact directly, you can tap the + (plus sign) button to the right of the To field to choose one of your contacts. After putting in your first contact, if you want to send this message to additional contacts, just start typing in a new name and the list will pop up again for you to choose the next contact that you want to send this message to. You can also carbon copy (CC) additional contacts. Next, you'll want to key in a subject in the Subject field and then your message in the body field below. Your email can be as long as you like. Once you have your message addressed and composed, you can tap the Send button to send it. If you tap the Cancel button, you'll be given the opportunity to save it as a draft and continue it later.

Emailing a Photo

The iPhone has a built-in 2-megapixel camera and it supports syncing photos from your computer. You can email either the photos you take with the iPhone's camera or the ones that are already in your iPhone's Photo Library. To email a photo, go to the Home screen by pressing the Home button and then tap the Photos button. If you want to send a photo that you took with your iPhone's camera, then it will be in the Camera Roll folder. If you want to send a photo that you synced from your computer, then it will either be in the Photo Library or one of the albums that you brought over. Find the photo you want to send and tap on it. In the lower-left corner will be a rectangle with an arrow coming out of a box. Tap that button and you'll have the choice to Use as Wallpaper, Email Photo, or Assign to Contact. You want to tap the Email Photo option. This will put your photo into the body of a new message. You can then address the message to the contact or contacts that you want to send the photo to, give it a subject, and even key in some text in the body area. After you've got your message worded the way you want and addressed to your contact(s), just tap the Send button to send it off.

Emailing a Note

The iPhone has a Notes application and you can email any of the notes that you create. To email a note, tap the Notes button from the Home screen. If you have more than one note, you can navigate to the note you want to email by tapping the left or right arrows at the bottom of the Notes screen. Once you find the note you want to email, tap the Envelope button and this will copy your note into the body of a new email message. You can now address it to the contact(s) that you want to send it to. It also uses the note's title as the subject, which you can change if you want to. You can add or delete part of the note if you only want to send a portion of it or add to what was there. Once you have the email addressed, tap the Send button to send it on its way.

---

iTip

Not only can you email someone photos and notes, but you can also email someone a URL directly from Safari. While in Safari on the page that you want to send the URL for, tap the Address Bar and you will see a Share button in the upper-left corner. Tap the Share button and it will generate a new email message with the URL of that page in the body. All you have to do is address the email to your contact(s) and tap Send.

Header Details

When you receive an email, you might want to see the details of who the message was actually addressed to. When you view a message, you'll see the word "Details" next to the From address. Tap Details to reveal all the names/email addresses of the people that the original message went to. Tap Hide to hide the details again.

iTip

If you tap one of the addresses in the Details area, including the sender, and they are not already one of your contacts, you will get the ability to create a new email to that person, as well as add them to your contacts.

Switching Between Accounts

If you have two or more email accounts set up on your iPhone, you can switch between them to view messages in each account's Inbox. Tap the Mail button on the Home screen and then if you're not already on the Accounts screen, you can get to it by tapping the Accounts button in the upper-left corner. Once you get to the Accounts screen, you can tap on any of your accounts to view email in that account.

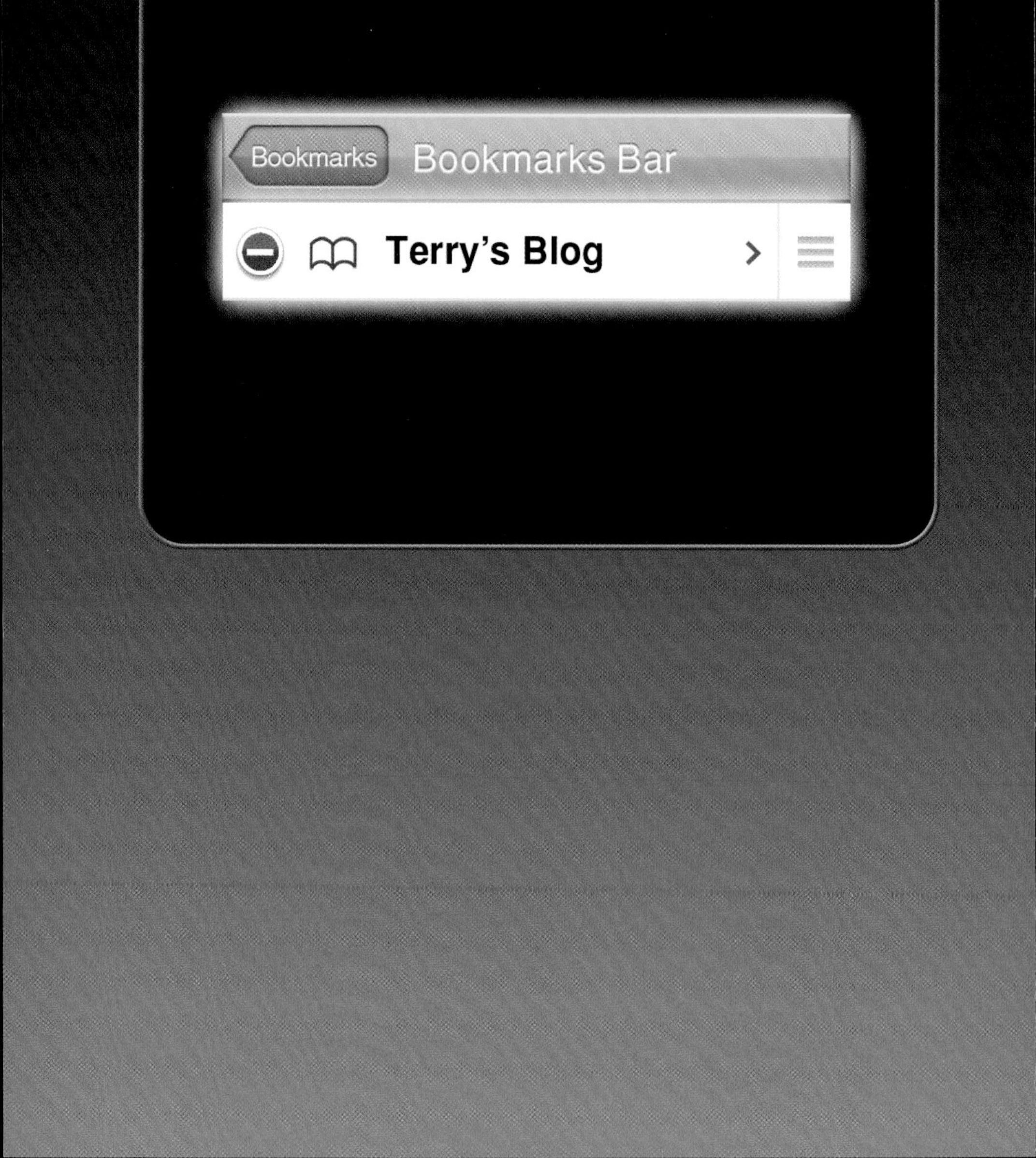
Bookmarks
Bookmarks Bar
Terry's Blog

Chapter Four

Surfin' Safari

Using the iPhone's Safari Web Browser

 Now you gotta admit—the Beach Boys' classic hit "Surfin' Safari" is just about as perfect a title for a chapter on using the Safari Web browser as you can get. But as you know, that's where the cohesiveness ends on this page, because the rest of this paragraph really has nothing to do with browsing the Web, or safaris, or even the iPhone for that matter. That's right, this is my "special time" where you and I get to bond on a level that I normally reserve only for close personal friends and men's room attendants. You see, when someone has read as much of this book as you have, a very magical thing happens. It's a magical moment of extreme clarity we both share simultaneously (but not at the same time), and although we experience this together, we do it totally separately, but still as one (which isn't easy to do). For example, it's that moment when you realize that you've already invested so much time in this book that you really can't stop now and you're "in it for the long haul." For me, it's the moment when I realize that you've had the book so long now you can't really return it for a refund. You see, it really is magical. So, put down the book, and take just a moment to close your eyes, breathe deeply, and just let your mind drift off to a place where it doesn't matter that the chapter introduction doesn't actually relate to the content in the coming chapter. That type of thing no longer matters to you because in your mind you're finally free—free to finally reach out and touch that existential neo-ocular nirvana that can only happen in Seattle. I have no idea how to end this gracefully. Hey! Quick—look over there!

Launching Safari

SCOTT KELBY

Safari is the iPhone's Web browser. It is by far the best Web browsing experience on a mobile phone to date. Safari will launch automatically when you tap on a URL (Web address) in one of the other applications. However, if you want to launch it manually, it's easy. Go to the Home screen and tap the Safari button at the bottom of the screen. The first time you launch Safari it will launch to a blank screen.

---

iTip

Your Web and email connections will be much faster if you can jump on a wireless net-work (at home, at the office, at your local coffee shop, etc.), but finding a free wireless connection when you're on the road is a lot trickier, unless you know this trick: Go to Maps from the Home screen, and type in "wifi," then a comma, and the city and state you're in (i.e., wifi, Kennebunkport, ME), and it will pinpoint the location of nearby free Wi-Fi coffee houses, restaurants, etc. There's also a website called JiWire Wi-Fi Finder, which looks and acts like an iPhone application, and can search not only local free spots, but any open Wi-Fi network. Check it out at http://iphone.jiwire.com.

Keying in a URL Manually

Once Safari is up and running, there will be an Address Bar at the top of the screen. You can tap in the Address Bar to bring up the keyboard. From there you can key in the URL of the website that you want to go to. There is even a ".com" button on the keyboard to help you complete your URL. Once you have the address keyed in, you can tap the Go button to go to it. If you want to type in another URL and there is one already there, you can clear it by tapping the X in a gray circle to the right of the address once you tap on the Address Bar.

 iTip

It's usually not necessary to key in the full address, such as http://www.creativesuitepodcast .com. Usually just keying in the domain name and the domain extension will work, such as creativesuitepodcast.com.

Navigating a Webpage

Once you get to the webpage that you keyed in the URL for, you should know the best ways to navigate within Safari. First, to scroll down the page you actually use your finger to flick the page up. Undoubtedly, in most cases the page will be too small to read. You can quickly zoom in on a page by double-tapping on the page. This will zoom the display nice and large. To move the page around, just use your finger to drag the page in the direction that you want to drag it in. To zoom out, double-tap the page again. You can also zoom in and out on a page using multi-touch. To zoom in on the page, use two fingers in a spreading out motion as if you're expanding the size of the page to zoom in. To zoom out on the page, use your two fingers to pinch the page as if you're making it smaller, because you are. As you navigate to different links, you can go back to a previous page by tapping the left-facing arrow at the bottom of the Safari screen. You can go forward by tapping the right-facing arrow.

iTip

Even when you're zoomed out on a page that is too small to read, the iPhone's Safari Web browser does an amazing job of letting you tap on links. I'm amazed at how accurate it is when I tap a button that I can barely read—it still knows where I'm trying to tap and takes me there. If you've scrolled down a long page, double-tapping on the time at the top of the screen will take you back up to the top of the webpage.

Using Your Bookmarks

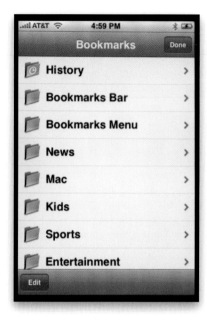

While keying in URLs can be fun, and good practice for the iPhone's keyboard, you'll probably want to take advantage of Bookmarks to get to your favorite sites. The iPhone automatically syncs your Bookmarks from Safari on your Mac or PC, or your Favorites in Internet Explorer on your PC. To use one of these Bookmarks on the iPhone, tap the little book button at the bottom of the Safari screen. All of your Bookmarks will be listed just as they appear on your computer. They'll be in the same folders and in the same order. Navigate to the Bookmark you want to use and tap it to go to that site.

---

iTip

Although the iPhone offers the best Web viewing experience on a mobile phone, you may find it slow loading some of the more graphic intensive sites when you're not con- nected to Wi-Fi. Some of your favorite companies may offer a "mobile" version or low bandwidth version of their site so that you can get to the information you need without all the fluff. For example, check out http://mobile.fandango.com as opposed to http:// fandango.com. You'll see that it gives you just what you need to see movie times and even buy tickets without loading all the pretty graphics.

Adding a Bookmark

Although the iPhone uses the same Bookmarks that are on your computer, you may discover a new site that you'd like to bookmark while you're out with your iPhone. If you have a page open in Safari that you'd like to bookmark, tap the + (plus sign) to the left of the Address Bar. This will prompt you to name the Bookmark, which you can simply leave as the name of the page as it appears. Or you could rename or shorten the name to your liking. You can also determine where it saves the Bookmark in your Bookmarks folder structure by tapping on the Bookmarks button below the URL. Once you're happy with the name and location of the Bookmark, tap the Save button to save the Bookmark.

iTip

I check movie times at my local AMC theater fairly often, and if you do the same, you'll love this website that looks, acts, and feels just like an iPhone application from Apple (even though it's actually a website). Just to go www.moviesapp.com, enter your zip code, choose your local theater, and you'll swear you're using an application (rather than a website). It has movie times, each movie's running time, you can watch the movie trailers, and you can even buy your tickets right there. You'll love it!

Editing a Bookmark

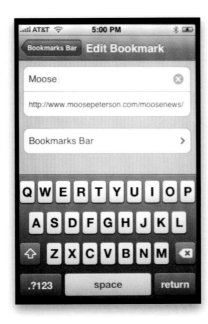

Sometimes website addresses change and you need to update your Bookmark. One great thing is that if you update a Bookmark on your computer, it will update in the iPhone the next time you sync. However, if you want to update it right on the iPhone, you can. Launch Safari and tap the Bookmarks button at the bottom of the screen. This will bring up your Bookmarks list and you'll be able to navigate to the folder containing the Bookmark you want to edit. Next tap the Edit button in the lower-left corner of the Bookmark folder screen. Then tap the Bookmark you wish to edit. You'll be able to edit the name and the URL, as well as the Bookmark location. Once you've made your changes, tap the Bookmark folder button in the upper-left corner of the screen to return to the list of Bookmarks. You can then tap the Done button when you're done making edits.

Deleting a Bookmark

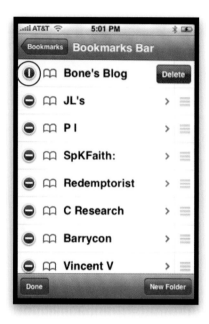

If you have a site bookmarked that you no longer need, you can delete it right from your iPhone. With the Safari application open, tap the Bookmarks button to bring up your list of Bookmarks. Navigate to the folder screen that lists the Bookmark that you wish to delete. Tap the Edit button in the lower-left corner and each Bookmark will have a – (minus sign) in a red circle to the left of it. Tap the red circle and then a Delete button will appear for that Bookmark. Tap the Delete button and that Bookmark will be deleted forever.

Using Google or Yahoo Search

It's great to be able to go to sites that you already know by either keying in the URL or using your Bookmarks. However, it's even more fun sometimes discovering new sites. You can search for sites right on your iPhone using two of the industry's leading search engines. The iPhone is set to Google's search engine by default. However, if you prefer Yahoo, you can make Yahoo the default by changing your preference in the Safari settings (tap on the Settings button on the Home screen). To use your default search engine, launch Safari from the Home screen. Then tap the Address Bar to bring it up along with the keyboard. Now tap on the search field and type in your search terms. Once you've typed in your search terms, tap the Google (or Yahoo) button on the bottom right of the keyboard to begin your search. Once your search results come up, you can then tap on any of the links to go to any of the pages that you want to visit.

iTip

Notice the Share button in the upper-left corner above the Address Bar. When you tap this button, it will create a new email with the URL that was in the Address Bar in the body of the email message. This way you can send someone a Web address with a single tap.

Viewing Your Pages Horizontally

The iPhone has an amazing feature that automatically detects when the iPhone is rotated 90° in either direction. This works great in Safari to allow you to view your pages in a horizontal view. Depending on the layout of the page, this could mean not having to scroll or zoom in as much. To use this feature, simply navigate to the page you want to view horizontally in Safari. Then hold your iPhone up (the sensor doesn't work so well when the iPhone is lying down) and rotate it 90°. The display will automatically refresh with the new orientation. You can use all the same options while in this mode, including the keyboard.

---

iTip

If you press-and-hold your finger down on a text link or graphic link on a webpage, a little pop-up window will appear showing the URL that the link will take you to.

Dialing a Phone Number on a Webpage

Oftentimes we search for companies on the Web not only to research them, but also to call them. If you search for a company in Safari or navigate to any page that has a phone number on it, chances are the iPhone will recognize that phone number as a phone number and it will be highlighted in blue. You can tap the phone number and the iPhone will ask you to confirm whether or not you want to dial it. If you tap Call, you'll be taken to the Phone application automatically, where your call will be placed. Once you tap End Call, you'll be returned to Safari to the page you were last viewing.

Navigating Back and Forth

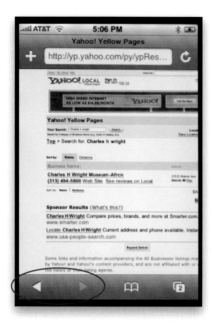

Safari on the iPhone supports two ways of browsing: The first way is the traditional browsing method that as you tap on links on a page, the page you are currently viewing is replaced by the new page. This is how every browser that you've ever used works. The other way is a cross between spawning new pages and the tabbed browsing you're used to in Safari or Internet Explorer on your computer. When you tap a link on a page in Safari on your phone, Safari goes to that page by replacing the page you were currently looking at. To go back to the previous page, tap the left arrow at the bottom of the Safari screen. Once you go back at least one page, you can go forward by tapping the right arrow.

---

iTip

If you're on a webpage that is long and requires scrolling, you can of course flick your finger to scroll the page, or you can double-tap to zoom in on the page and then double-tap in the lower half of the page to scroll down a screen at a time (just be sure to tap in a blank area of the page).

Getting a New Page

Sometimes you may want to keep viewing the page in Safari that you're looking at and have the flexibility of going to a different page without losing the current page. To do this, tap the little Pages button in the lower-right corner of the Safari screen. This will shrink your current page down and a New Page button will appear in the lower-left corner. Tap the New Page button to create a blank page in Safari. Now you can either key in a new URL, do a search, or use your Bookmarks to go to the page you want to go to.

iTip

The next time you're typing a Web address into the Address Bar using the keyboard, take a quick glance at the Spacebar. That's right—there is no Spacebar (because Web addresses don't use spaces), but in its place is a one-button shortcut for .com, plus a Forward Slash key, and a Period key (all handy stuff you need when entering Web addresses).

Navigate Between Pages in Safari

Once you have two or more pages open in Safari, you can navigate back and forth between them. To go to another open page in Safari, tap the Pages button in the lower-right corner of the Safari screen. Then, by flicking your finger across the page towards the left or the right, you can navigate between your open pages. Once you get to the page you want to view, just tap it to bring it back up to full screen. This is really handy when you're trying to compare things such as prices or schedules between two different sites at once.

iTip

Want to add a great game of blackjack to your iPhone (it's not really an application—it's a website that looks and acts just like an Apple-created iPhone application, but it's actually just a website)? Then go to http://mynumo.com/iphone/bj/blackjack.htm.

Refreshing a Page

Safari does a good job of keeping the page you're currently viewing in place when you switch between applications. However, if you're finding that you want to know the latest bid on that eBay item you're watching, you may need to refresh the page. You can refresh just about any page in the Safari browser on the iPhone by tapping the circular arrow button in the upper-right corner of the Safari window to the right of the Address Bar. This will cause Safari to go out to the Web server for the page you're viewing and grab the latest version of it.

Viewing RSS Feeds on the iPhone

The Safari browser on the iPhone does support RSS (Really Simple Syndication) feeds. Most news sites, blogs, and corporate sites today provide RSS feeds so that users can subscribe to them and check the feed rather than constantly going directly to the site to see if it's been updated. Some sites actually have the links to their various RSS feeds right on their homepages. However, it's easier to bookmark and organize these feeds on your computer rather than doing it on the iPhone. On your computer, use Safari (available for both Mac and PC) and go to some of your favorite sites. You will see an RSS button in the upper-right corner of the Address Bar. Click the RSS button to take you to the feed page for that particular site. This is the page you'll want to bookmark. I place all my RSS feeds in a folder called (wait for it) RSS on my Bookmarks Bar. When I'm on the iPhone, I can tap any feed in that folder to see all the current headlines for that site.

Filling in an Online Form on Your iPhone

At some point you're going to go to a website in Safari on your iPhone that requests some type of information. You could be placing an online order at your favorite etailer or simply keying in your username and password on your favorite community site. When you get to a form on a webpage, you can tap on the first field on that page, which will zoom in on the field and bring up the keyboard. You can type out your response for the first field, and then if the second field is still in view, you can just tap it and keep typing. If the next field is not in view, you can tap Done on the keyboard, which will zoom the page back out again and then you can tap the field you want to go to next and the keyboard will reappear. If you tap on a pop-up menu on a page, Safari does something very cool: it magnifies the list of choices and puts them in a flick wheel that you can spin with your finger to get to the right option. Once you've got your form all filled out, you can dismiss the keyboard by tapping Done and then tap the submit button for your form to submit your data.

Closing a Page

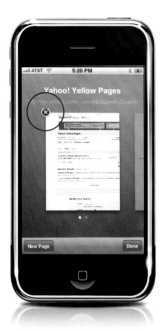

Having multiple-page support in Safari is awesome. However, when you're finished viewing a page, there is no reason to have it out there hanging around. To close a page in Safari that you no longer need open, tap the Pages button in the lower-right corner of the Safari screen. Navigate to the page you wish to close and tap the little red X in the upper-left corner of the page. The page will close and you'll be switched to a page that is still open.

MMS Support—Kind Of

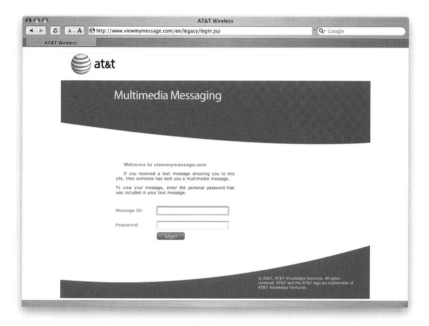

The first iPhone doesn't support MMS (multimedia messaging), so there is no way to send a photo, for example, directly to another cell phone without using email. Although Apple may add this feature in a future update, there is no way to send an MMS message on the original iPhone. However, if you receive an MMS message, AT&T has stepped in with a solution. AT&T has a website set up at www.viewmymessage.com. When you receive an MMS message on your iPhone, you'll get a text message stating that you can't display the message on the iPhone, but it will also give you the viewmymessage .com site with a special login and password just for that message. You can then view the message directly in Safari on the iPhone.

Chapter Five
Tool Time
iPhone's Tools for Organizing Your Life

 Are we now to the point that our lives have become so complex, so chaotic, and so congealed (congealed?) that the only way to keep track of it all is to buy a hand-held device which becomes the center around which our lives revolve as it shouts out alarms, and commands us to be in certain places at certain times? All this while we're trying to monitor the markets, and stay in contact with people on different continents, in different time zones, and the only way we feel we can find the location of the nearest coffee shop is to send a request to a satellite in geosynchronous orbit above the earth requesting that it not only point out the location of said coffee shop, but that it ping a different satellite to provide a detailed photographic image of its roof? Is this what we've come to? Yes, yes it is, but I'm totally okay with it. Why? Because I bought stock in numerous GPS satellite companies, Google, and Starbucks. Okay, I really didn't buy stock in those companies but I could have, and I could have done it right from my iPhone. Well, at least until my wife found out, because at that moment you would've heard that cast-iron sound of a frying pan connecting with a husband's head (the one you hear in cartoons), but it would've been so loud that they would've heard it aboard the International Space Station (which is in a geosynchronous orbit high above the earth, by the way), and when the astronauts heard it, they'd look at each other, nod, and say, "I bet some guy's wife just found out he bought a whole bunch of stock using his iPhone." You know, it really is a small world after all.

Setting Up Clocks for Different Time Zones

If you do business internationally, or just in different times zones (I know, they're kind of the same thing), then you can set up world clocks to show the time in each city. Start at the Home screen and tap on Clock. Then tap on World Clock at the bottom-left corner of the screen to bring up the World Clock screen. By default, it shows the current time in Cupertino, California. To delete Cupertino as one of your cities, tap the Edit button in the upper-left corner, and a red circle with a – (minus sign) appears before the word "Cupertino." Tap that red circle once and a Delete button appears on the right. Tap Delete and it's gone (the clock—not Cupertino itself). To add a new city, tap the + (plus sign) button in the top-right corner to bring up a city search field. Type in the city you want to add (in our example here, I typed in Rome, Italy. Actually, I just typed in R-O and Rome, Italy, appeared in the list). When your city appears in the list, just tap on it and it's added as a clock. To add more cities, just tap the + (plus sign) button again.

---

 iTip

Why does the default time in the World Clock screen show Cupertino, California? It's because that's where Apple's headquarters (also known as "the mothership" to Macintosh fanatics) is located.

Using the Stopwatch

I love this stopwatch feature because it's just so simple, efficient, and it has a really large readout. To get to it, start at the Home screen and tap on Clock. Then tap on Stopwatch at the bottom of the screen to bring up the Stopwatch screen. There are only two buttons: Start and Reset. To start timing something, tap the green Start button. Once the stopwatch starts running, the green Start button is replaced by a red Stop button. To start over, tap the Reset button. If you want to record lap times, just tap the Lap button (what used to be the Reset button before the stopwatch started running), and those times are listed in the fields below the two buttons. You can have lots of individual lap times (I stopped at 32 laps—man, was I tired), and you can scroll through the list of lap times just like you would scroll any list—by swiping your finger on the screen in the direction you want to scroll.

---

iTip

When you're looking at the time in a World Clock screen, if the clock's face is white, that means it's daytime in that city. If the clock's face is black, it's night.

Setting Up a Countdown Clock

If you need to count down a particular length of time (let's say you're cooking and you need to know when it's been 12 minutes), then you can set a countdown timer to alert you after 12 minutes has passed. To do this, start at the Home screen and tap on Clock. Then tap on Timer at the bottom-right corner of the screen to bring up the Timer screen. You can scroll the Hours and Minutes wheels onscreen to set the amount of time you want to count down to. Just below the countdown wheels is a button called When Timer Ends, and this is where you choose either the ringtone that your iPhone will play when the countdown clock hits zero, or you can choose to have the iPhone simply go to sleep (which is great if you want to play music for a specific amount of time before you fall asleep, and then have the iPhone put itself to sleep to save battery life while you're sleeping). Once you've set your countdown time, and selected what happens when the timer hits zero (by tapping the When Timer Ends button), just tap the green Start button and the countdown begins.

Using Your iPhone as an Alarm

You don't have to take that travel alarm clock with you on the road anymore, because your iPhone has a great alarm clock built right in. Start at the Home screen and tap on Clock. Then tap on Alarm at the bottom of the screen to bring up the Alarm screen. To add an alarm, tap on the + (plus sign) button up in the top-right corner of the screen. This brings up the Add Alarm screen where you can choose a variety of options, including whether, and how often, to repeat this alarm, what sound will play when the alarm goes off, whether to allow you to snooze the alarm, and the name of the custom alarm you just created (that way, you can save custom alarms, which is handy if you have to wake up at different times on different days. You can have one alarm for home, one for travel on weekdays, one for travel on weekends, etc.). When you've configured your alarm the way you want it, tap Save and your alarm appears in your Alarm list, and it's turned on. At the designated time, your alarm sounds (and will keep sounding) until you tap on one of two buttons that now appear onscreen: (1) Snooze (if you turned that feature on), or (2) OK. If you tap Snooze, the alarm sound stops, but it will re-sound in 10 minutes. If you tap OK, it turns the alarm off. Also, if you want to activate an alarm you've already created, you can turn on/off alarms in the Alarm list. To turn on a particular alarm, tap the gray button. To turn it back off, tap the gray button again.

Using the Calculator

It's not a fancy calculator, but it's simple and the buttons and readout are quite large (it makes you feel like you're using a regular hand-held calculator). To get to the Calculator, start at the Home screen and tap on Calculator. The Calculator then appears, and you use It lIke any other calculator—by tapping on the keys.

Finding Videos on YouTube

You can watch videos from the wildly popular online video sharing site YouTube.com right from your iPhone. It doesn't actually download the videos from YouTube.com onto your iPhone—you search for videos you want to watch, and then you watch them on your iPhone just like you would watch YouTube.com videos on your computer. However, you can bookmark your favorite videos and get right to them. Start at the Home screen and tap on YouTube. Then tap on Search (at the bottom of the screen) to bring up a search field. Tap on the search field to bring up the keyboard, type in your search term, then tap the Search button to search YouTube's vast video library. The results appear in a list below the Search field. To watch one of these videos, just tap on it, then turn your iPhone sideways (videos always play in this wide mode). To see more about a video in the list, tap the blue arrow button to the right of the video in the results list.

Playing YouTube Videos on Your iPhone

When a video first starts playing, a set of video controls appears onscreen for pausing the video, adjusting the volume, etc. There's even a button to email a YouTube video link to a friend. To bring back those controls, just touch the screen. To return to the search results list, press the blue Done button in the top left corner.

Saving YouTube Videos as Favorites

To bookmark a video you like (so you can jump directly to it next time), tap on the Bookmarks button in the video controls (at the bottom of the screen while it's playing) or the Bookmark button beneath the video's info (to the left of the Share button when you're done playing the video). Also, at the bottom of the YouTube screen are buttons that take you directly to the featured videos of the day, YouTube's most viewed videos, and videos that you've bookmarked. If you tap the More button, you'll see a new set of menus which let you jump to YouTube's Most Recent videos, see their Top Rated videos, or see a History (list) of the YouTube videos you've already watched.

Customizing the YouTube Buttons

Although a default set of buttons appears in a bar at the bottom of the main YouTube screen, you can customize this bar to contain the YouTube buttons you use the most. To do this, start at the Home screen and tap YouTube, then tap the More button. When the More screen appears (and you see the row of buttons across the bottom), tap the Edit button in the top-right corner of the screen to bring up the Configure screen. Now you just press-and-hold your finger on any button you'd like to appear on your bar, and simply drag it down to the bar and hold it over the button you want to replace. The button to be replaced gets a large white glow around it, and once you see that, you simply take your finger off the screen and your new button appears in that spot. That's all there is to it.

---

iTip

If you're staying in a hotel out of town, here's a helpful tip: go to Maps, enter your hotel's name, city, and state, tap Search, and when Maps pinpoints your hotel on the Map, tap on the blue arrow to the right of your hotel's name to see its info. In that Info screen, tap the button for Add to Bookmarks, then give your bookmark a name and tap Save. Now, anytime you need directions back to your hotel, just go to Maps, tap the Directions To Here button, tap in the End field, then tap the Bookmarks button. Choose your hotel's name, and it inputs the exact address for you. Of course, you can do this same thing with your home, office, or any common starting or ending point.

Using Maps to Find Just About Anything

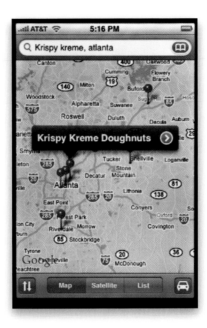

The iPhone's built-in Maps feature is pretty darn amazing: it lets you instantly find anything from the nearest golf course to a dry cleaner in the next city you're traveling to, and can not only give you precise directions on how to get there, it can call your destination as well. Here's how to use it: Start at the Home screen and tap on Maps. When the Maps screen appears, you'll see a search field at the top where you can enter an address you'd like to see on the map. For example, let's say you'd like to find the nearest Krispy Kreme donut shop (not that I would actually ever search for one. Wink, wink). You'd tap once on the search field to bring up the keyboard, then you'd type in the name of the business, followed by a comma, then the city, then tap the Search button. In the example shown above, I entered "Krispy kreme, atlanta" and a Google map appeared with red pushpins on seven locations in the Atlanta area. If you tap on one of those pushpins, a little pop-up appears with the name of that location. If you tap the blue arrow button in that pop-up, it takes you to an Info screen for that particular location. If you tap the phone number, it dials it for you (that way you could call and ask, "Is the Hot Now sign on?" Ya know, if you were so inclined).

iTip

If you're using Maps and you want to toggle between finding an address and getting driving instructions between two addresses, press the blue button in the bottom-left corner (the one with one arrow pointing up, and one arrow pointing down).

Getting Driving Directions

 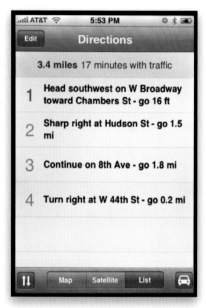

You can use the iPhone's Maps feature to get step-by-step driving directions to any location, and from any location. Here's how: Start at the Home screen and tap on Maps. Let's say you want directions to my favorite restaurant in the whole world—Carmine's at 200 W. 44th Street In New York City—and let's say you're staying at the Cosmopolitan Hotel: Tribeca at 95 W. Broadway, also in New York City. At the top of the Maps screen, tap on the search field to bring up the keyboard (if there's already an address in the search field, tap the little X in the gray circle on the far-right side of the search field to clear the last entry) and type in 200 W. 44th Street, New York, then tap the Search button. When the map appears, tap on the little blue arrow button on the far-right side of the pop-up address marker to go to the Info screen for that address. Now tap the Directions To Here button, which brings up a Start field for you to enter the address of where you are now (which is the Cosmopolitan Hotel: Tribeca, so you'd enter 95 W. Broadway, New York) then tap the Route button. This displays the route from your hotel to Carmine's on the map, but for the step-by-step driving instructions, you'll need to tap the List button, and it shows the step-by-step driving directions (as shown above right). It also displays the distance in miles and how long the drive should take considering traffic. By the way, Carmine's is very popular so if you're going (and it's in your Contacts list), while you're in the Info screen, tap the phone number to have your iPhone dial Carmine's so you can make reservations. Otherwise, you'll be waiting an hour or more for a table.

Finding Your Contacts on the Map

If you've included a street address for your contact, you're just a couple of taps away from seeing their house on the map. Just go to the All Contacts list, tap on their name, and when their Info screen appears, tap once on their address. This automatically takes you to the Maps feature and pinpoints their address on the map. Better yet, once the map appears, tap on the Satellite button and it shows you a satellite photo of their house. To zoom in for a closer look, just double-tap on their location on the screen. Each double-tap will zoom you in that much closer.

iTip

In the Maps application, if you're having the map give you directions from one loca-tion to another, it's usually helpful to tap the List button (at the bottom-right corner of the screen) so you see a street-by-street, turn-by-turn list of the directions. But that's not the tip. The tip is: if you tap on any of those directions, it instantly switches back to Map view to pinpoint exactly where that list item appears on the map between the two locations.

Seeing Your Local Weather

You can set up your iPhone so you're only one tap away from seeing your current local weather, and a six-day forecast as well. Start at the Home screen and tap on Weather. This brings up the weather forecast for (you guessed it) Cupertino, California (by the way—it's pretty much always sunny and around 72 degrees. I'm surprised anyone lives anywhere else). Anyway, you can change it to give your local weather by tapping once on the little "i" button in the bottom-right corner of the screen. This brings up the Weather screen, where you'll see Cupertino listed with a little red circular button with a – (minus sign) in it. Tap on that button and a Delete button will appear to the right of Cupertino. Tap that Delete button and it deletes the weather for Cupertino. (By the way, there are two buttons at the bottom of this screen so you can choose to display your weather in Fahrenheit or Celsius—just tap on the one you want.) To add your own city's weather, tap on the + (plus sign) in the top-left corner to bring up the Add Location screen. Using the keyboard at the bottom of the screen, type in your city and state, or city and country (in the example shown here, I typed in "Safety Harbor, Florida"), then tap the Search button. It will then display your city in the list (provided, of course, that it found your city), and all you have to do now is tap on your city name, then tap the blue Done key in the upper-right corner, and now you're just a tap away from your local weather.

Adding Weather for Other Cities

To add the weather for additional cities, you start out pretty much the same way as shown on the previous page—tap on that little "i" icon at the bottom of your local weather screen, and when the next screen appears, tap the + (plus sign) up in the left corner of the screen to add a new city. Type in the city and state (or city and country), then tap the Search button. When it finds your city, tap on it, then tap the Done button. Although it's added, you won't see it when you first tap the Weather button. You have to slide your finger on the screen (just like you do with photos in the Photos application) to see other cities you're monitoring. So basically, you slide your local weather out of the way, and the next city slides into place. To return to your local city, slide back in the opposite direction. By the way, on the bottom-left corner of each weather forecast screen is a little Yahoo! logo. Tap on that logo, and it takes you to a Yahoo! webpage with information about that city, including a city guide, today's calendar of events, photos, and more.

 iTip

The color of the Weather screen lets you know whether it's day or night in the city you're looking at. If the Weather screen appears in blue, it's daytime, and if it's a dark purple, it's night.

Making Quick Notes

There's a Notes feature for taking quick notes you want stored on your iPhone. To get there, start at the Home screen, then tap the Notes button. When the Notes screen appears, you'll see a list of any notes you've already taken. If you haven't created any notes yet, it figures you're there to create a new note, so it takes you to (no big surprise) the New Note screen. Type in your note (using the keyboard at the bottom of the screen), then tap the Done button in the upper-right corner when you're finished. This hides the keyboard and displays your note full screen. To return to your list of notes, tap the Notes button in the top-left corner. To read any note in the list, just tap on it (each note automatically displays the date and time it was created at the top of the note). To delete a note, tap on it, then in the next screen tap on the Trash button at the bottom of the screen.

---

iTip

In the Notes application, to quickly edit an existing note, just tap on it in the Notes list. Then when the note appears full screen, just tap anywhere on the note, and the keyboard appears—ready for editing. When you tap, if you tap on a word, your cursor appears right on that word. If you want to add to a note, tap just below your text.

Getting Stock Quotes

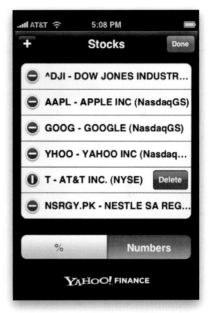

You can monitor the current quote for stocks in your portfolio directly from your iPhone. Start at the Home screen, then tap the Stocks button. When the Stocks screen appears, by default it shows the the Dow Jones Industrial Average, along with a default list of stocks (Apple, Google, Yahoo, AT&T, and Nestlé). You can delete any of these and add your own stocks to monitor by first tapping on the little "i" icon in the bottom-right corner of the screen. This brings up a list of the current indexes and stocks being monitored with a red circular – (minus sign) button before each listing. Tap on the red minus sign button for the stock you want to remove and a Delete button appears to its right. Tap the Delete button and that stock is removed. To add a new stock (or index), tap the + (plus sign) button in the upper-left corner, which brings up the Add Stock screen. Type in the company name, index name, or stock symbol (if you know it) on the keyboard, then tap the blue Search button at the bottom-right corner of the screen. When it finds your company, it will display it in the list. Tap on the company name and it's added to your list of stocks. To add more stocks, tap the plus sign button again. When you're done, tap the blue Done key in the upper-right corner. You can add as many stocks as you'd like, and to see other listings just scroll down the screen by swiping (Apple calls it "flicking") your finger from the bottom of the screen up.

Getting More Info on Your Stocks

To see a chart of your stock's performance over time, just tap on the stock and a graph will appear at the bottom of the screen. To change the time frame of the chart, just tap on the list of time frames at the top of the chart (they range from 1 day to 2 years). For even more information on your currently selected stock, tap on the little Yahoo! logo that appears in the bottom-left corner of the Stocks screen, and it takes you to a Yahoo Finance webpage with detailed information about the company, including recent news articles. To return to your Stocks screen, press the Home button, then tap on Stocks.

iTip

To toggle between displaying the stock price's gain or loss in number and the gain/loss as a percentage, just tap directly on the numbers themselves (if the stock is showing a gain, the numbers appear with a green background. If the stock is showing a loss, the background is red).

Importing Your Calendar

The iPhone has a built-in calendar application, and depending on which calendar program you're using on your computer, you can import your calendar directly into your iPhone (or you can manually add info to your calendar directly from your iPhone, as you'll learn on the next page). You can import calendar info from either Apple's iCal or Microsoft Entourage on the Macintosh (see Chapter 9 for how to set up Entourage), or if you use Windows, you can import your calendar from Microsoft Outlook. As long as the calendar on your computer uses one of the applications just noted, when you connect your iPhone to your computer for syncing, it will upload your calendar information directly into your iPhone automatically (if you have the preference set). To see your imported calendar info, start at the Home screen and tap the Calendar button. You can view your calendar as one long scrolling list or in a more traditional calendar view. To view by day, tap the Day button at the top of the screen, or tap Month to view the entire month (as shown here). In the Month view, if you see a small dot appearing below the date, that means you have an event scheduled for sometime that day. To see the event, tap once directly on that day and that day's events will appear below the calendar. If you tap the Day view, it shows you the entire day by time, starting at 12:00 a.m. In Day view, you can navigate to other nearby dates by tapping the left or right arrow buttons near the top of the screen. Any time you want to jump to today's calendar, just tap the Today button in the top-left corner of the screen.

Adding Appointments to Your Calendar

To add an appointment to your iPhone's calendar, you could of course just add it on your computer and then sync your iPhone and your computer, but if you need to manually enter an appointment, it's easy. Start at the Home screen, then tap Calendar. In the Calendar screen, press the + (plus sign) button in the upper-right corner of the screen to bring up the Add Event screen. To give your event a name, tap on the Title field and the keyboard appears so you can type in a title (and a location, if you like). Tap Save, then tap on the Starts/Ends field to set the time when your appointment (event) starts and ends. This brings up the Start & End screen. It chooses Starts by default, and you can choose the start time for your event by using the scroll wheels at the bottom of the screen. Then tap the Ends button and choose the ending time. If this event runs the entire day, turn on the All-Day button by tapping on it. When you're done, tap the blue Save button. When you return to the Add Event screen, there are also options for repeating this appointment (for example, let's say you have a company meeting every Monday at 9:00 a.m.—you can tap Repeat, and when the Repeat Event screen appears, you can choose Every Week, and it will add that event to your calendar every Monday at 9:00 a.m. automatically). If you'd like iPhone to give you a reminder alarm before your appointment (or event), tap the Alert button. In the Event Alert screen that appears, tap how long before the event you want the alarm to go off, then tap the Save button at the top of the screen. When everything's just the way you want it, tap the blue Done button in the top-right corner.

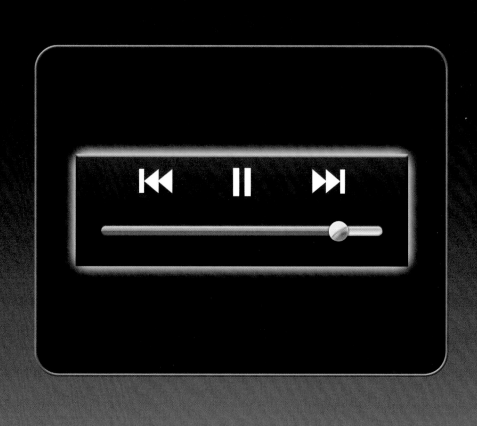

Chapter Six

The Song Remains the Same

Using iTunes and the iTunes Store

 Any chapter that is named after a Led Zepplin movie from 1976 has to get some special credit in rock 'n' roll heaven, right? This is another movie I never saw, but I'm pretty sure it had Jimmy Stewart and Ann Margaret in it at some point. Didn't it? Anyway, this chapter is about how to use iTunes and the iTunes Store (which used to be called the iTunes Music Store until Apple added TV shows and movies, and then it seemed silly to still call it a music store, especially when it had huge hit movies in it like *Star Trek: The Wrath of Khan* [that was with Leonardo DiCaprio and Ellen DeGeneres, wasn't it?] and *Zoolander* [with Meryl Streep and David Niven, I believe]). Anyway, here's the thing: in this chapter I will endeavor to help those who (a) have never had an iPod, and thus (b) never used iTunes, which means you've (c) never been to the iTunes Store, which means (d) you're not a teen, because every person between the ages of 13 and 19 has to report to the iTunes Store as part of the government's Selective Service Online Shopping Act of 1984, which stipulates that every male child over the age of 14 must stare directly and blankly into a hand-held video game device for no less than nine hours per day (including a mandatory two hours during school). As I was saying, this chapter is for people who need a quick course on what iTunes is, what's in the iTunes Store (and how to buy stuff there), and then how to get that stuff into their iPhone without any person between the ages of 13 and 19 ever looking up from their screen. This, I think we can do.

Importing Songs from CDs

Chances are if you haven't been using an iPod up to this point, most of your music collection is still on CDs. Luckily, getting them into iTunes (and from there into your iPhone) couldn't be easier. Start by launching iTunes (remember—you have to have at least iTunes version 7.3 or higher to sync with your iPhone. If you don't, go to Apple's website and download the latest version). When iTunes appears, put a music CD into your computer's CD/DVD drive, and a dialog will appear asking if you'd like to import the songs on your CD into the iTunes Music Library. All you have to do is click the Yes button, and iTunes does the rest—importing each song, in order, with the track names—for you. It puts these songs into your Music Library mixed in with all your other songs (see "Creating Music Playlists" on page 124 for how to keep these songs separate).

---

iTip

If you have an Internet connection when you go to import a music CD, iTunes will go to the Web, cross reference the name of your CD with an online music database, and in most cases, it will automatically add the track names to all of your songs. If it couldn't find your CD in its vast database, you must have some mighty obscure musical taste, and I mean that in the most nonjudgmental, totally disingenuous way possible.

Buying Songs from the iTunes Store

You buy iPhone-compatible music from the iTunes Store (the iTunes Store is the single largest online music retailer in the world today) and to enter the store, just click on iTunes Store in the Source list on the left side of the iTunes window. Although you can jump directly to different genres (like Rock, Hip-Hop, Country, Pop, etc.) and browse through there, the quickest way to find the music you want is to do a search using the Search field in the upper-right corner of the iTunes window. Here I entered "Black Eyed Peas," then hit the Return (PC: Enter) key on my keyboard, and in just seconds all the Black Eyed Peas albums and songs available on iTunes appeared (as seen here). You can buy (and download on the spot) individual songs for 99¢, or an entire album for vary- ing prices (the Peas albums go for anywhere from $9.99 to $11.99). To hear a 30-second preview of any song, just double-click on its title. If you want to buy a song, click the Buy Song button (circled above in red), and it's immediately downloaded to your computer (of course, before you can start buying and downloading songs, you'll have to take a moment and create an iTunes account, so do that now. No problem…I'll wait). Okay, so that's pretty much the scoop—you can use the Search field to find just the song(s) you want, or you can click the Home button (that little icon that looks like a house just below the Volume slider on the top-left side), and browse through iTune's huge collection of songs (there are more than a million). Any songs you buy are added to your Music Library and they'll also appear under Purchased in the Source list.

Creating Music Playlists

So, you've imported some songs from CDs, and you've bought a few songs from the iTunes Store, and they're all there together in your Music Library (if you go to the top of the Source list on the left side of the iTunes window and click on Music, you'll see every song you have in iTunes). The way you keep things organized is by creating playlists, which are basically collections of your favorite songs. So, for example, if you wanted to create a collection of nothing but your favorite rock songs from the 1980s, you would start by clicking on the + (plus sign) button at the bottom-left corner of the iTunes window. This adds a new blank playlist to your Source list, and its name is highlighted so you can type in a name (how about "Big Hair Bands Playlist"?). Once you've named your playlist, press the Return (PC: Enter) key on your keyboard to lock in the name of your playlist, then make sure you clicked on Music in the Source list to show your entire iTunes Music Library of songs. Now, scroll through your music collection and each time you run across one of your '80s rock favorites, click-and-drag that song onto your Big Hair Bands Playlist in the Source list. A green circle with a + (plus sign) in it appears to let you know that you're adding a song to that playlist (as seen here). Once you've gone through and added all your big hair favorites, you're only one click away from hearing just those songs (and you'll be able to transfer this new playlist to your iPhone). Also, once your songs are in a playlist, you can click-and-drag them into the order you'd like them to appear. To delete a song from a playlist, just click on it and hit the Delete (PC: Backspace) key on your keyboard (this doesn't delete it from your Music Library, just from that playlist).

Creating Smart Playlists

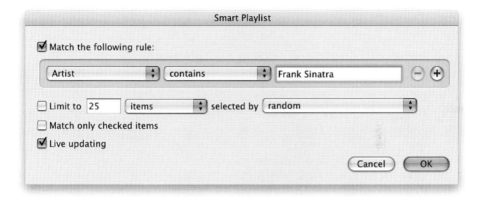

If you don't want to take the time to make a bunch of different playlists (actually, making your own custom playlists is half the fun of using iTunes), you can have iTunes do most of the work for you. iTunes already comes with some of these "Smart Playlists." For example, you'll see playlists already created with the 25 songs you've played the most, the songs you've played most recently, and if you rate your songs in iTunes (using the 1- to 5-star rating system), you'll see a Smart Playlist with only your top-rated songs. To create your own Smart Playlist, just press-and-hold the Option key on a Mac, or the Alt key on a PC, and click the + (plus sign) button at the bottom-left corner of iTunes. This brings up a dialog that asks you to choose the criteria for your new Smart Playlist. So, let's say you've imported three or four different Frank Sinatra CDs, and you've bought some Sinatra songs from the iTunes Store. When your Smart Playlist dialog appears, you can have it search your entire Music Library and build a playlist of all your Sinatra songs for you (as shown above). These Smart Playlists are incredibly powerful, yet easy to use—you just choose your criteria from the pop-up menus. Let's try another: want all of your country music songs in one playlist? Change the Artist field to Genre, erase "Frank Sinatra" and type in "Country," then click OK. To narrow your criteria even further, click the gray + (plus sign) button to the right of the text field (where you typed "Country") to add another line of search criteria.

Downloading Radio & Video Podcasts

Podcasts are free radio or TV shows produced by individuals or companies on a wide range of topics, from teaching you how to cook, to teaching you martial arts, to shows that are just comedy, or product reviews, or news. Everyone from ESPN to National Geographic, from HBO to NPR (radio) and about everybody in between offers free downloadable podcasts, which you can subscribe to (also for free) and they're downloaded to your computer (and then onto your iPhone, if you choose) as soon as each episode is released (some are daily, some post weekly episodes, some bi-weekly, etc.). To find a podcast that interests you, go to the iTunes Store, and on the homepage click on Podcasts. There are podcasts on the Podcasts main page, and you can search through different categories (like Sports & Recreation, Technology, Health, etc.). When you find one you like, you can click the Get Episode button to download just an episode, or click the Subscribe button to download each episode as they're released for free (you can unsubscribe any time).

---

iTip

I host a weekly video podcast called Photoshop User TV *(along with my co-hosts Matt Kloskowski and Dave Cross), and each week we share Adobe Photoshop techniques, tips, news, and step-by-step tutorials. Each episode is approximately 30 minutes and we have an awful lot of fun (and millions of downloads each month around the world). You can find it on iTunes by searching for* Photoshop User TV.

Buying TV Shows and Movies

Besides buying music, now you can also buy full-length movies, TV shows, and music videos from the iTunes Store and you can watch these on your iPhone as well. From the iTunes Store homepage, in the navigation list at the top left of the main window, click on either Movies, TV Shows, or Music Videos. When your choice appears, you'll find featured titles. For example, if you chose TV Shows, you would see the entire seasons of TV shows from ABC, NBC, CBS, FOX, and more than 60 broadcast and cable channels (individual episodes cost $1.99 each, but you can buy an entire season of a show—every episode which aired that year—for around $35). Movies have their own section on the iTunes Store as well, and full-length movies run from around $9.99 to $14.99 for the most part.

iTip

Playlists aren't just for music—you can create your own custom playlists for your favorite TV shows or movies (so you could have a playlist of just scary movies, or a playlist of classic TV shows). You create them just like you would a music playlist.

Choosing What Goes into Your iPhone

Since iPhones don't have as much storage space as your computer does, you wouldn't want to put all of your movies, podcasts, and TV shows onto your iPhone at once (you'd probably run out of room), so iTunes lets you choose which music playlists, which TV shows, and which movies get uploaded. You do this by connecting your iPhone to your computer, and then in iTunes, in the Source list on the left side of the window, click on your iPhone to bring up its preferences in the main window. You'll see a row of tabs along the top of the main window for Music, Photos, Podcasts, Video, etc. For example, click on the Video tab, and when the Video preferences window appears (shown here), in the TV Shows section at the top of the screen, instead of choosing to sync All TV Shows, choose Selected TV Shows instead. Then in the list of TV shows you have in iTunes, only check the shows you want uploaded to your iPhone. You can choose to upload all unwatched shows, or just the three most recent, five most recent, etc. This way you can control which shows, and how many, are uploaded to your iPhone. Once you make your changes, be sure to click the Apply button in the lower-right corner of the iTunes window (it's circled here in red).

Going from iTunes to Your iPhone

Now all it takes to get music, movies, podcasts, music videos, and TV shows from iTunes into your iPhone is to connect your iPhone to your computer. iTunes will automatically launch (once you connect your iPhone) and it will immediately start uploading just the music playlists and videos you chose on the previous page. That's all there is to it.

---

iTip

We have just scratched the surface of what you can do in iTunes and the iTunes Store. If you're into this kind of stuff, I know a guy who wrote a killer book on iTunes, the iPod, and the iTunes Store. His book is called (ready for this?) The iPod Book (from Peachpit Press), and I have to say, it looks pretty much like this book. In fact, this book is based on the layout and design of that book. But I won't get in trouble because I'm the author of that book, too! (Aw come on, you knew that was coming, right?)

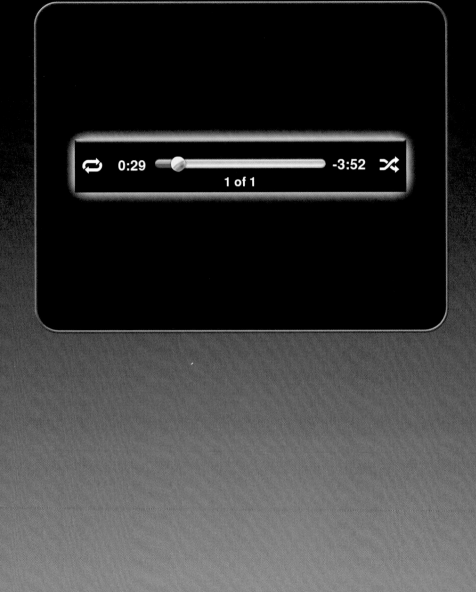

Chapter Seven

Video Killed the Radio Star

Using the iPhone's Built-In iPod

 It's hard to believe, but the 1979 song "Video Killed the Radio Star," from The Buggles, actually has an important place in music history because when MTV went live back in August 1981, their debut music video was (you guessed it) "Video Killed the Radio Star." I have a regular iPod that does play video, but it doesn't have the larger, more luxurious widescreen display the iPhone has, and it was while pondering that thought, I realized the iPhone itself was playing a role in music history, and as an iPhone owner, like MTV, I would have to choose which music video would debut on my iPhone. Knowing that my choice would, in some small way, be part of my own personal music history really put a lot of pressure on me. I mean, think about it—years from now it's quite possible that sociology students at colleges in far off places, like Helsinki and Cincinnati, might one day study, debate, and pick apart my music video debut choice, and I'm not sure I can deal with that kind of responsibility. And that's probably why, when I was carefully scrolling through my music video collection, rather than "flicking" or "swiping," I accidentally tapped the Play button right when the Spice Girls' "Wannabe" video was scrolling by, and I swear it felt like I went into some kind of slow motion dream state as I scrambled and fumbled to tap the Pause button…but it was too late. There it was, playing full screen. My only solace was, like The Buggles, the Spice Girls are British. If you listen carefully, you can almost hear the university professors in Helsinki giggling as they type their fall course descriptions.

Syncing Your iTunes Library

When you connected your iPhone to set it up and activate it, you had preference tabs in iTunes for Music, Podcasts, and Video. These tabs allow you to control which songs, play-lists, podcasts, and videos get synced to your iPhone. Since the iPhone has limited capac-ity, it is quite common to have more content on your computer than your iPhone will hold. Therefore, it's best to create playlists and rules for how things get synced to your iPhone. If you haven't already, create some playlists of your favorite tunes—the ones that you'll really want to listen to while you're on the go (this is covered in detail in the iTunes chapter of this book). When it comes to podcasts and videos, you can not only specify which shows/movies get synced to your iPhone, but you can also specify things like only sync unwatched episodes or the most recent ones. When you watch them on your iPhone, the next time you sync your iPhone to your computer, iTunes will mark them as watched and sync the next most recent or unwatched episodes. Once you change your settings in iTunes for what will be synced with your iPhone (by clicking on a tab, turning on the Sync option, and choosing your settings), you can click the Apply button to save the settings and initiate an immediate sync.

Launching the iPod Application

Unlike other iPods you may have used, the iPod on the iPhone is an application. To launch it, press the Home button at the bottom of the iPhone and then tap the iPod button. This will take you to the iPod application, which will allow you to play your music and video files that you synced from iTunes. Although you launch the iPod application, you don't have to stay in it just to listen to your content. Once you start a song, podcast, or audiobook playing, you can switch to other iPhone applications, such as Mail or Safari, and the iPod will keep playing your audio.

Navigating the iPod

By default, when you launch the iPod application on the iPhone, at the bottom of the screen you will have buttons for Playlists, Artists, Songs, Videos, and More. These buttons allow you direct access to those areas. You can jump back and forth between these areas at any time to access your content in the way that you want. You'll likely use Playlists most often. However, if you've got a tune stuck in your head and you want to play it immediately, then you could tap the Songs button and go right to your list of songs. Since it is possible to have literally thousands of songs on your iPhone, the list could be quite long. You can jump to a specific letter of the alphabet by tapping on the letter you want to jump to along the right edge of the list.

---

iTip

If you want to see how many songs you have on your iPhone, tap the Songs button and scroll down to the bottom of the list. You can see your song count listed there.

Playing Your First Song on the iPhone

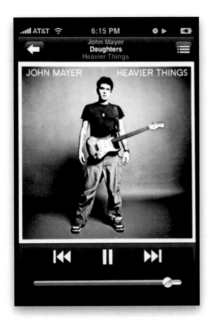

If you're like me, you'll want to check out the iPod application on the iPhone pretty quickly. So tap the iPod button on the Home screen and then either tap Playlists, Artists, or Songs to find the first song that you would like to hear. Once you locate your song (probably something like "Bad to the Bone"), just tap it to begin playing it. Since the iPhone has a built-in speaker, you'll actually hear the sound come from the iPhone's speaker if you don't have headphones plugged in. If the song has album art, it will be displayed while the song plays. If there is no album art, then the iPhone will just display a default music note while the song plays. If you want to pick a different song, you don't have to stop or pause the current song. Just tap the left arrow button in the upper-left corner of the iPod screen to return to your Songs list. Once your song finishes, the iPhone will automatically play the next song in the list. To conserve battery life, the iPhone's display will go to sleep while the song is playing. To get back to the iPod, just press the Home button and unlock the iPhone by swiping your finger across to the right on the Slide to Unlock button.

Adjusting the Volume

There are two ways to adjust the playback volume on the iPhone. The first way is using the onscreen volume slider that is at the bottom of the iPod screen. Just use your finger to drag the knob (circle) to the right to make the playback louder or to the left to lower the volume. The other way to adjust the volume is to use the physical volume buttons on the left side of the iPhone. These are the same buttons that you use to adjust the ringer volume and call volume, too.

Using Your Playlists

The idea of playlists is what separated the iPod from most other MP3 players back in 2001. So it's only natural that the iPhone would have great playlist support. Playlists are created on your computer in iTunes. You can pick and choose which playlists get synced to your iPhone from iTunes. Once you go to the iPod application from the Home screen, you will have a Playlists button. Tap this button to see your available playlists on the iPhone. When you tap on any of your playlists, you'll see the songs contained in that playlist. Tapping any song will begin playing that song. The subsequent songs in the playlist will play in order. The great part about playlists is that you can have as many as you want with no real storage penalty. The same song(s) can be in multiple playlists but not take up additional space on the iPhone. For example, let's say you have a playlist called Male Vocals and one called Quiet Storm. Both playlists could contain John Legend's "Ordinary People" track. However, that track will only be copied to the iPhone once, no matter how many playlists it's in. So go nuts creating any playlists that might suit your mood at any given time.

Shuffle Your Songs

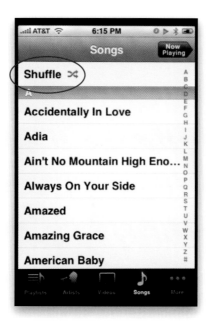

It's great to be able to listen to your songs in the order that you placed them in your playlist. However, it's often more fun to let fate decide which song is going to play next. This way you're constantly surprised because you don't know what's coming next. You can play your songs in order by tapping on any song in any playlist. However, if you want the songs in a particular playlist to play randomly, tap Shuffle at the top of the playlist instead. Shuffle will be at the top of any playlist of songs that contains two or more songs. This will pick the first song at random and play the rest of the playlist in random order.

Playing Songs by Artist

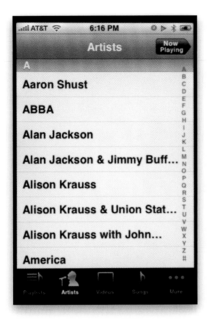

I'm in the mood to hear some Earth, Wind & Fire, but I didn't create a specific playlist to hear their music. No worries. The iPod application on the iPhone lets you play songs by specific artists. From the iPod's main screen, tap the Artists button. You will then see a list of all your artists. From this list, you can tap the specific artist that you want to hear. Then you'll see a choice between All Songs and the individual albums that you have from that artist. (*Note:* If you only have one album from that artist, then you'll just see the songs.) You'll see this list of albums even if you don't have all the songs on any of the given albums. You can now either tap All Songs to see a list of all the songs you have by that artist or you can tap a specific album to just play the songs on that album. Either way, you'll be able to play the songs in order or tap Shuffle (provided you have two or more songs) to play the songs at random.

Fast Forward or Rewind Through a Song

There are some songs that you can listen to over and over again and never get tired of them. However, there are some songs that you can listen to a certain part of the song over and over again, or there's a certain part of the song that you can't stand. Either way, there is a way to "scrub" through a song that is playing. Of course, in order for this to work, you have to start a song playing. So tap the iPod button on the Home screen, choose a song by playlist, artist, or song and start playing it by tapping on it. You will either see the album art for the song, or a music note if there is no album art for that song. In either case, tap the screen right on the artwork. This will display a progress bar at the top of the screen. As the song plays, the little knob on the progress bar will be advancing to the right. You can tap right on that knob and drag it left to go back in the song or right to move forward through the song.

Repeating Playback of a Song or Playlist

If you want to hear the same playlist or song over and over again, you can turn on the Repeat feature in the iPod application. Start playing the song that you want to repeat or a song from the playlist that you want to repeat. Tap on the album art and you'll notice a little circular arrow button to the left of the progress bar. This allows you to turn on Repeat. There are three modes to Repeat: Tapping the Repeat button once will repeat the entire playlist after all the songs have been played. Tapping the Repeat button again will show the circular arrow Repeat button with a 1 on it. This means that the current song will repeat over and over until you stop it. Tapping the Repeat button one more time will turn Repeat off.

Advancing to the Next Song

You can advance to the next song by tapping the double arrows that point to the right beneath the album art of the currently playing song. You can also go to the previous song by tapping the double arrows that point to the left. However, there's an even cooler way to advance to the next song. The iPhone comes with a pair of earbuds that also double as a hands-free headset for making calls. There is a little microphone on the right earbud cable. That microphone is also a button that will advance to the next song while you're listening to music on your iPhone. To advance to the next song, press this button (squeeze it) twice quickly.

Pausing Playback

Although you're in the groove now, you will want to be able to pause the iPod playback from time to time. The good news is that there are a few ways to do this: First off, if you receive a call, the iPhone will automatically pause the iPod playback until you complete your call, and then pick right back up where you left off. The second way to pause playback is to do so right on the iPod screen. Tap the Pause button at the bottom of the screen. Lastly, if you're listening to your content with the supplied Apple iPhone headset, you can press the microphone button once to pause playback. To resume playback, just press the button again.

Using Cover Flow

Cover Flow gives you a visual organic way of flipping through your music collection. This feature first appeared in iTunes 7 and now the iPhone's iPod application is the first iPod to get this feature. To use Cover Flow, tap on the iPod button on the Home screen. Once you're in the iPod application, simply hold up your iPhone and rotate it 90° in either direction. This will automatically switch the display to Cover Flow. You will now see your album art (or the music symbol). You can flick or drag your finger across the screen to move through your albums. Once you find an album that you're interested in drilling down further on, you can tap it and it will flip over to reveal the songs on that album. You can tap any song to play it. The playback will be limited to the songs on that particular album. You can flip the album back over again by tapping the name of the album at the top.

---

iTip

You can also flip albums over and back by pressing the little "i" button in the lower–right corner of the Cover Flow screen.

Playing Other Songs from the Same Album

While it's great to be able to access all the songs of a particular album while you're in Cover Flow view, you can also access songs from the same album as the song that is currently playing. Start any song playing in the iPod application that has at least two songs from the same album. Now tap on the album art. This will flip the album over and reveal the other songs that are on that album. You can start playing any song you want on that list without having to go find it elsewhere.

Rating Your Songs on the iPhone

iTunes has some really slick features that take advantage of song ratings. For example, you can create Smart Playlists that contain your top-rated tunes. While it's great that you can rate the songs as 1- to 5-star right in iTunes, it's sometimes more convenient to rate songs right on your iPhone while you're out and about. The next time you sync your iPhone to iTunes, the ratings you made on the iPhone will be applied to your songs in iTunes. To rate any song that is currently playing, tap the Track list button in the upper-right corner of the album art. The album art will flip over and you will see either five dots or the current rating that the song has. You can then tap the appropriate star/dot to rate your song as 1- to 5-star. Once you're done rating it, just tap the little Album Art button in the upper-right corner to return to your album art display.

Taking Advantage of Podcasts

Podcasts are a great way to keep up on the topics that you're interested in while you're on the go. There is a huge library of both audio and video podcasts in the iTunes Store, and the best part is that they are usually *free* to subscribe to. You can watch or listen to podcasts right in iTunes, but more importantly you can watch or listen to them on your iPhone. Once you've downloaded or subscribed to a podcast or two, you can then choose to have those episodes sync to your iPhone from iTunes. Once you have some podcast episodes on your iPhone, you can get to them from the iPod application. Tap the More button on the bottom-right side of the iPod screen and then tap Podcasts. You'll see your podcasts listed by show, and from there you can tap on a particular show to choose an episode to listen to. Tap it and away you go. If you listen to it all the way through, the next time you sync to iTunes it will mark it as heard and therefore remove it from the iPhone. Or it will remember where you left off.

 iTip

Hey, if you're looking for a couple of great podcasts to subscribe to, check out Scott's Photoshop User TV *and Terry's* Adobe Creative Suite Video Podcast: *www.photoshopguys.com and www.creativesuitepodcast.com. You can subscribe to both of these video podcasts right in iTunes.*

Watching Videos and Movies on the iPhone

Apple has done a good job supporting video playback on the iPhone. Using the iPod application you can watch movies, music videos, and TV shows that you purchase from iTunes *or* ones that you create yourself. You can also watch video podcasts. To watch a video, tap the Videos button at the bottom of the IPod screen. Your video content will be organized by Movies, TV Shows, Music Videos, and Podcasts. Tap the video you want to play and it will automatically play horizontally. So just rotate your iPhone to watch it. The video will play full screen. You can access the playback controls while it's playing by just tapping the screen. There are two screen modes: full screen and widescreen. To toggle between these modes, double-tap the screen. In widescreen mode, you'll see the entire video from edge to edge. If the video is at a different aspect ratio, then it may be presented with black bars at the top and bottom or left and right. You can also play it full screen so that there are no bars, but some of the video may be cropped off.

---

iTip

You can convert your movies into the proper format right in iTunes. Add the movie to iTunes and choose Convert Selection for iPod from the Advanced menu. Another hot tip: You can delete videos directly from the iPhone to make more room. Tap the Videos icon and flick your finger across the title of the video to expose the Delete button. Tap Delete to delete the video from the iPhone immediately.

Audiobooks

Audiobooks are great to listen to on the go. Unlike songs, the iPhone remembers where you left off, whether you started listening to the audiobook in iTunes or on your iPhone. Therefore, you can feel free to listen in either place and the next time you sync to your computer, iTunes will update the audiobook to remember where you left off. The iTunes store has a wide variety of audiobook choices. To listen to an audiobook on your iPhone, tap the More button at the bottom of the iPod screen. Then tap Audiobooks. Tap the audiobook you want to listen to to begin playback. The Next/Fast Forward and Previous/Rewind buttons will advance to the next chapter or go back to the previous chapter.

iTip

Although there is a Podcasts button on the iPod's More screen, it's audio only! If you have a video podcast and you want to actually watch it instead of just listening to it, tap the Videos button to see it listed there in the Podcasts section at the bottom.

Create an On-The-Go Playlist

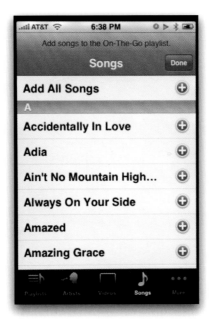

At some point, you may want to create a playlist while you're away from your computer. The songs are already on your iPhone, but you want to put them in a particular order right then and there. The iPhone supports creating playlists on the fly. They're called On-The-Go playlists. To create an On-The-Go playlist, tap the Playlists button at the bottom of the iPod screen. The first item in the list is the On-The-Go playlist option. Once you tap it, you'll be presented with a list of all your songs. Each song will have a + (plus sign) to the right of it. You can just tap the plus sign for each song that you want to add to the On-The-Go playlist. As you tap each song, it will gray out to indicate that it has been added. When you're done adding songs, tap the Done button and your new On-The-Go playlist will be ready for use. If you want to edit it, you can tap the Edit button in the upper-right corner of the On-The-Go playlist screen and you can then change the order of the songs by dragging on the List icon to the right of the song you want to move, or you can delete songs from the list by tapping the little red circle on the left side. You can also add additional songs by tapping the plus sign in the upper-left corner of the screen. When you're done editing, tap the Done button in the upper-right corner of the screen.

Receiving a Call While Listening to the iPod

Apple did a great job of integrating the Phone application with the iPod application. When you receive a call, the music will fade and you'll hear your phone ring. The iPhone will give you the choice of answering the call or declining it (which will send the caller to voicemail). If you answer the call, then you'll be taken to the iPhone's call screen. Once you end the call, the iPhone will pick up right where it left off playing your song or other media.

---

iTip

If you're listening to the iPod via the supplied stereo headset, you can also answer the call by clicking the microphone button on the right headset cable.

Using External Speakers or Headsets

Since the iPhone has a great iPod built into it, it stands to reason that you may want to connect your iPhone to some speakers to get the party rolling. The iPhone does have a standard 30-pin iPod dock connector on the bottom of it. It also has a stereo headphone jack on the top, but there are some caveats. Since the iPhone is a GSM based phone, its built-in "radio" could interfere with your stereo or speakers. When you plug your iPhone into a speaker system built for the iPod (not for the iPhone), you may get a message that says "This accessory is not made to work with iPhone. Would you like to turn on Airplane Mode to reduce audio interference (you will not be able to make or receive calls)?" You have the choice of turning on Airplane mode or not. What this simply means is that while in Airplane mode, the phone and Bluetooth portions of the iPhone are turned off so as not to interfere with your stereo speakers. However, while in Airplane mode you will not be able to make or receive calls. So you might want to try it on your speakers without going into Airplane mode. If there is no interference, you're home free. You can also use the iPhone Dock that came with the iPhone. It has a stereo line out port that can be used to connect directly to your stereo system. If you want to use your own headphones you can, but there may be an issue actually plugging them in. The iPhone's headset jack is recessed and therefore your headset plug may not be skinny enough to fit down in there. Luckily, both Belkin and Griffin Technologies have made adapters.

Setting a Sleep Timer

You can actually have your iPhone's music lull you off to sleepy land by setting a "sleep timer." A sleep timer will play your music until the timer expires and then it will put the iPhone to sleep. To set a sleep timer, first go to your iPod application and start playing the songs you want to play until the timer goes off. You can use a playlist (such as your "sleepy land" playlist—I know you have one—or any other playlist on your iPhone). Then press the Home button to go to the Home screen. Now tap Clock and then tap Timer. You can set the minutes, or hours and minutes, that you want the iPod to play before going to sleep. Next tap the When Timer Ends button and choose Sleep iPod. Then tap the Set button in the upper-right corner of the screen to return to the Timer screen. Now tap Start to begin the countdown. When the timer reaches the end of its set time, the music will fade and the iPhone will go to sleep.

Rearranging Your iPod Buttons

The first time you go to the iPod application you'll see buttons at the bottom of the screen for Playlists, Artists, Songs, Videos, and More. When you tap the More button, you'll see that you have a lot more options, such as Albums, Audiobooks, Compilations, Composers, Genres, and Podcasts. However, if you use any of these more often than the default buttons on the main iPod screen, you can swap them. For example, I rarely use the Songs button, but I use the Podcasts button all the time. So rather than having to keep pressing the More button to get to Podcasts, I put the Podcasts button in place of the Songs button. To move a button from the More screen to the main iPod screen, tap the Edit button in the upper-left corner of the More screen. You'll then see icons for all the other iPod categories. Simply drag the icon you want to move over the top of the button at the bottom that you want to replace with it, and when the existing button highlights, you can let go. You can tap Done when you've completed your edits.

---

iTip

While you're choosing which buttons you want to be your primary iPod buttons, you can also drag the ones that are there in a different order. For example, on my iPhone they are now listed as Playlists, Artists, Videos, Podcasts, and More. Just simply drag them in the order you want them listed.

Syncing Your iPhone with Another Computer

If you have your music on one computer and your contacts and calendar on another, you'll be happy to know that the iPhone does sync to more than one computer. For example, I work primarily on my MacBook Pro notebook. However, I have a desktop iMac that serves as our media jukebox. So I sync my contacts, calendars, bookmarks, email accounts, and photos from my MacBook Pro and my music, videos, audiobooks, and podcasts from the iMac. Here's how to do it: Sync the iPhone first to the computer that has your data on it—in other words, your contacts, calendars, etc. Uncheck all the things in the Music, Podcasts, and Video tabs (photos can be synced from either computer). Once the sync is done from the first computer, then head over to the other computer and launch iTunes. Don't plug in the iPhone just yet. After iTunes is up and running, then go to the iTunes preferences, click on the iPhone icon, turn on Disable Automatic Syncing for All iPhones, and click OK. Now you can plug in your iPhone to this computer and when it shows up in the Source list, you can uncheck all the data stuff and enable syncing of all the media stuff. Once you've got the appropriate boxes turned on, you can then hit the Apply button in iTunes to sync your media. From now on, the iPhone will sync data from the first computer and media from the second computer.

Chapter Eight

One Hour Photo

Enjoying Photos on Your iPhone

 I chose the movie *One Hour Photo* as this chapter's title after realizing that my song title choices were pretty much either "Photos of Toast" by Ectogram or "Photos of Nothing" by Southeast Engine. I was leaning towards "Photos of Toast" until I heard "Photos of Nothing," and I knew right then I needed to find something more productive to do for a living other than searching the iTunes Store for songs that contain the word "photo." But I digress. I could have gone with two more obvious choices like "Photograph" from Ringo Starr or Def Leppard. Personally, I like Def Leppard's "Photograph" because I feel cooler lip syncing to them whilst holding a pool cue than I do when singing Ringo's song, which you want to avoid doing in any bar that has a pool table. Luckily that's not a big fear of mine because the odds of finding a jukebox with Ringo's "Photograph" on it (the one that starts with "Every time I see your face, it reminds me of the places we used to go. But all I've got is a photograph...") are less than winning the Powerball lottery. That's because Ringo just isn't very big with the pool hall crowd, which is by the way, a crowd that does favor Def Leppard for one simple reason: Def Leppard is in the Pool Cue Air Guitar Hall of Fame. Sadly, it wasn't for "Photograph"—it was for "Pour Some Sugar On Me" which would have made a great chapter name if the iPhone had either Pouring or Sugar Dispensing features. Sadly, it has neither. I know what you're thinking, "He should have gone with 'Photos of Toast.'" That's not what you were thinking, was it?

Getting Photos into Your iPhone (Mac)

If you're using a Mac, the easiest way to get photos into your iPhone is using Apple's iPhoto application (which comes preinstalled on all Macs). You drag-and-drop your photos right onto the iPhoto icon in your Mac's onscreen Dock and it imports them into your iPhoto Library. Then, click on the + (plus sign) on the bottom left to create separate photo albums (like one for family shots, or one for travel photos, one for your portfolio if you're a serious photographer, etc.), and drag-and-drop photos from the Library right onto the album of your choice. Once your photos are arranged in albums within iPhoto, when you connect your iPhone to your computer, it automatically uploads your photo albums to your iPhone. You can see your uploaded albums by starting at the Home screen and tapping on the Photos button in the top row.

iTip

You can set up your iPhone so only certain iPhoto albums are uploaded to it. You do this when your iPhone is connected to your computer, which launches iTunes. Once iTunes is open, on the left side, under Devices, click on the iPhone to bring up the iPhone preferences. Click on the Photos tab, and you'll see that the default setting has all of your iPhoto albums being uploaded. If you'd like to choose just specific albums to be uploaded, click on the Selected Albums radio button and then turn on the checkbox beside the albums you want uploaded. When you've got just the ones you want uploaded turned on, click the Apply button in the bottom-right corner of iTunes.

Importing without iPhoto (Mac)

If you don't want to use Apple's iPhoto application to manage the photos you want uploaded to your iPhone, you can just put them in a folder on your Mac, and have iTunes do
the uploading for you. Here's how: First, connect your iPhone to your computer, which
brings up iTunes. In the Source list on the left side of the iTunes window, under Devices,
click on the iPhone icon to bring up the iPhone preferences, then click on the Photos tab.
At the top of this window, it says Sync Photos From, and from this pop-up menu, select
Choose Folder. This brings up a standard Open dialog, where you choose which folder
your photos are in. Once you navigate your way to that folder, click the Choose button,
then go to the bottom-right corner of the iTunes window and click the Apply button to
upload the photos in that folder to your iPhone. Easy enough.

Getting Photos into Your iPhone (PC)

There is no version of Apple's iPhoto application for Windows, but luckily it supports direct automatic importing from two other photo management applications: (1) Adobe Photoshop Album (which is a free application—you can download it from www.adobe.com/products/photoshopalbum/starter.html). Or (2) any version of Adobe Photoshop Elements since version 3. To set this up, first connect your iPhone to your computer, which brings up iTunes. In the Source list on the left side of the iTunes window, under Devices, click on the iPhone icon to bring up the iPhone preferences, then click on the Photos tab. At the top of this window, it says Sync Photos From, and from this pop-up menu, choose which one of the two supported applications you want to import from—Photoshop Album or Photoshop Elements (3 or higher). Now click the Apply button in the bottom-right corner to upload the photos to your iPhone.

Importing without Album or Elements (PC)

If you don't want to use Photoshop Album or Photoshop Elements to manage the photos you want uploaded to your iPhone, you can just put them in a folder on your PC and have iTunes do the uploading for you. Here's how: First, connect your iPhone to your computer, which brings up iTunes. In the Source list on the left side of the iTunes window, under Devices, click on the iPhone icon to bring up the iPhone preferences, then click on the Photos tab. At the top of this window, it says Sync Photos From, and from this pop-up menu select Choose Folder. This brings up a standard Open dialog, where you choose which folder your photos are in. Once you navigate your way to that folder, click the OK button, then go to the bottom-right corner of the iTunes window, and click the Apply button to upload the photos in that folder to your iPhone.

Viewing Your Photos

SCOTT KELBY

Once you've imported photos into your iPhone, to see them start at the Home screen, then click on Photos. This brings up the Photo Albums screen and at the top is your Camera Roll (the photos taken with the iPhone's built-in camera), then your Photo Library (all the photos you've imported into your iPhone all lumped together), and then a list of any separate photo albums you created, like family photos, vacation photos, etc., using Apple's iPhoto application (on a Mac), or Photoshop Album or Photoshop Elements (on a PC), or by importing them from folders. To see your photos as thumbnails, tap on any album. You can scroll through your thumbnails by swiping your finger up/down the screen. To see any photo full screen, just tap on it. Once your photo is full screen, you can see other photos in that album at that size by swiping your finger on the screen in the direction you want to scroll. If your photo bounces like it's hitting a wall, you've reached the end of that album, so swipe back in the other direction.

iTip

If a photo is wide (in landscape orientation), to see that photo as large as possible, just turn your iPhone sideways, and the photo automatically adjusts so it's viewed horizontally. To see a vertical (portrait orientation) photo as large as possible, just turn your iPhone back upright.

Viewing a Slide Show

Start at the Home screen, then click on Photos to bring up the Photo Albums screen. To see any photo album as a slide show, just tap on the album, then when the thumbnails appear, at the bottom of the window is a Play button. Tap on it to start the slide show. To stop your slide show, just tap the screen once, then tap the name of your album that appears in the top-left corner of the screen. iPhone slide shows come complete with smooth, built-in dissolve transitions between each photo, but if you want to choose a different type of dissolve, or change the length of time each photo appears onscreen, then start at the Home screen and tap on Settings. When the Settings screen appears, tap on Photos, which brings up a list of options for your slide show. To change any setting, just click on it. You can also turn on Repeat to loop your slide show, or Shuffle to play your slides in a random order. When you're done, tap the Settings button in the upper-left corner.

Pausing and Manually Viewing Slide Shows

To pause a running slide show, just tap the screen. This not only pauses the current slide show, but it brings up an additional set of slide show controls at the bottom of the screen. They include left and right arrow buttons to manually advance your slides, a Play button to restart your slide show, and an Options button (on the bottom left) that brings up a pop-up menu which lets you choose the currently displayed photo as your startup wallpaper, email the photo, or assign the photo to a contact. At the top of the screen, it now displays which number photo you're currently on (for example, photo 2 of 9), and there's a button on the top left that lets you return to the thumbnail list of photos for that album.

---

iTip

If you're looking inside an album, and want to know how many photos are in it, without having to return to the main Photo Albums screen, just scroll all the way to the bottom of the thumbnails and it will display how many photos are in that album.

Adding Background Music to Your Slide Show

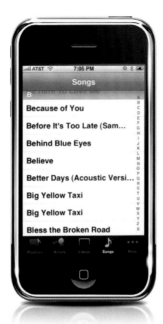

There really isn't a slide show feature that lets you include music (at least at this point), so we're going to do a workaround (it's a little clunky, but it works). Start at the Home screen, then click on the orange iPod button. In the iPod screen, tap on Songs and scroll to the song you want as background music for your slide show. Tap the song and the music starts playing (as long as you don't have your headset plugged in, you'll hear the music playing through your iPhone's built-in speaker). Now, press the Home button to return to the Home screen, tap on the Photos button, tap on the album you want to see as a slide show, then tap the Play button that appears at the bottom of the thumbnails screen. There you have it—your slide show playing with background music playing behind it.

iTip

To change the order of your photos, you have to go back to your computer. Change the order the photos appear in the album, then go to iTunes, sync your iPhone with your computer, and it will update your iPhone with the new order.

Using the Built-In Camera

SCOTT KELBY

To take photos with the iPhone's built-in camera, start at the Home screen and tap on Camera. This takes you to the Camera screen, and when you first get there you'll see what appears to be a closed shutter, but after just a couple of seconds, you'll see a full-color image of what you're pointing your iPhone at (the camera is on the back side of the iPhone—on the top left). To take a photo, tap the camera shutter button at the bottom center of the screen. Three things will quickly happen: (1) you'll hear a shutter sound, (2) you'll see the shutter graphic appear, like a shutter opening and closing, and (3) you'll see the photo you just took appear onscreen for about two seconds. Then it gets sucked down into the tiny icon on the bottom-left side on the screen, where it will remain until you tap on that little icon. So, tap on that little icon. This brings up the Camera Roll screen and this is where all the photos you've taken with the built-in camera are stored. To see any photo full screen, just tap on it. A set of navigation controls appears at the bottom of the screen, but disappears in a couple of seconds. To bring the controls back, just tap once on the photo.

Viewing Photos Taken with the Camera

To see photos you've taken with the built-in camera, start at the Home screen and tap on the Photos button to bring up the Photo Albums screen. At the top of the screen is the Camera Roll—these are the photos taken with the built-in camera, so tap on Camera Roll. This brings up the Camera Roll screen (shown above), with thumbnails of the photos you've taken. To see a photo full-screen size, just tap on it. To delete a selected photo, tap the Trash button at the bottom-right corner of the screen. (*Note:* If you don't see the Trash button, tap once in the center of the full-screen photo and the controls will appear on the bottom of the screen again.) To see a slide show of the photos in your Camera Roll, tap the Play button at the bottom of the screen. To use a photo as a wallpaper background, or to email it to a friend, or to assign it to a contact, click the button on the bottom-left corner and buttons for each of those tasks will appear onscreen—just tap the one you want.

Zooming In on Photos

To get a closer look at any photo, either in your photo albums or a photo you've taken with the built-in camera, just tap on the photo to see it full screen, then place your pinched fingers in the center of the screen and spread them outward to zoom in. To zoom in tighter, pinch-and-spread outward once again. To return to the normal-sized view, just double-tap on the screen.

Receiving Photos from a Cell Phone

Although the iPhone lets you email a photo to someone, it doesn't let you send a photo directly to someone else's cell phone. And if you want someone to send you a photo, they'll need to email it to you. However, what if someone takes a photo with their cell phone, and they send it directly to your iPhone—then what happens? Believe it or not, your iPhone gives you a message that you've received a multimedia message that cannot be read by your iPhone, and then it gives you a website where AT&T has posted the photo sent by your friend. They also give you a one-time username and password so you can go online and see the photo that was sent. It's really a very clever work-around. Except for one thing: you have to write down the website address and the username and password, because there's no direct link to the site, and no way to copy-and-paste the username and password. Hey, I said it was a very clever workaround—I never said it was perfect.

Making a Photo Your iPhone's Wallpaper

When you wake your iPhone from sleep, or when you're making a call, you can have a photo appear as your background image (for example, I like to see a photo of my wife and son every time I wake my iPhone—it just puts a smile on my face). To do this, start at the Home screen and tap on Photos. When the Photo Albums screen appears, tap on the album that contains the photo you want to use as your background wallpaper. Then when you see the thumbnails screen appear, tap once on the photo you want to use, then tap on the button in the bottom-left corner of the screen and a list of options pops up. Tap the Use As Wallpaper button and then a new screen appears where you can adjust the size and position of your photo by dragging-and-pinching to zoom the photo. When it looks good to you, choose Set Wallpaper, and you're set (sorry, that was lame).

How to Email a Photo

You can't just send a photo from your cell phone to someone else's cell phone, but you can email a photo to someone's email account. To do that, start at the Home screen then tap on the Photo button. If the photo you want to send is one you took with your built-in camera, tap on Camera Roll, then tap on the photo you want to email. If it's from one of your photo albums, tap on the album, then on the thumbnail of the photo you want to email. Either way, once the selected photo appears at full-screen size, tap the button on the bottom-left corner of the screen to bring up the options for what to do with that photo. Tap on Email Photo, which takes you to the New Message screen. Tap on the To field and the keyboard appears so you can enter the email address for your email (if the person you're emailing is in your All Contacts list, tap on the blue circle on the right side of the To field). You can tap on the Cc field (to send a copy to another email address) and the Subject field to enter the subject line for your email. You'll see that your photo is already included at the bottom of the email message, so once that info is entered, you can email your photo by tapping the Send button in the upper-right corner of the screen.

Chapter Nine

The Trouble with Boys

Troubleshooting Your iPhone

 Terry asked me to write this chapter intro for two reasons: (1) it's my job to write the chapter intros, and (2) I'm not really qualified to write anything in a troubleshooting chapter. It's only because nothing has gone the slightest bit wrong with my iPhone since I bought it, so I've never had an occasion to trouble-shoot a problem. On the other hand, Terry (being a renown gadget guru and committed iPhone freak) is very hard on technology. It's not unusual to stop at Terry's house and find him taking some new gadget (like an iPhone) and exposing it to harsher conditions than your average user is likely to experience (unless he or she were to lead an expedition to Antarctica, or do so many bad things that they wind up in "the really hot place" where really bad people go—you know where I'm talking about: Phoenix). Anyway, Terry asked me to write this intro, and I have to tell you, I'm honored to do it. In fact, I'm honored to be sharing the pages of this book with him, because even though many people don't know this, Terry is the reigning Midwest freestyle clogging champion (in the men's 35–45 age bracket), and he competes nationwide at clogging conventions, state fairs, and competitions, including Clogapalooza 2007 where he took third place in the men's individual freestyle competition. I was there cheering Terry on, and I've got to tell you—he was robbed. One of the judges worked for Microsoft and, not coincidentally, was the only one to score Terry's performance as an 8.2 (all the other judges scored him as a 10). What a shame—we really thought it was "his year."

Can't Connect to Your Wi-Fi Network

Networks requiring a password may sometimes not work on the iPhone. If the network is secured by Wired Equivalent Privacy (WEP), you might want to try entering the HEX key instead of the ASCII password. To do this, you first need to locate the HEX key for your network. If it's an Apple AirPort Base Station you can find it using the Apple AirPort Utility or AirPort Admin Utility and log into your base station. It's called Equivalent Network Password under the Base Station menu. If you have a third-party wireless router you'll have to log in using a Web browser and look up the HEX key for your particular router.

The iPhone Doesn't Come On

Make sure that your battery is charged. Try either connecting it to your computer's USB port or to the AC adapter that came with the iPhone. The iPhone's screen should come on when it's connected to a power source and indicate that the battery is charging. If not, then you may want to try a soft reset. Press-and-hold the Home button and the Sleep/Wake button located on the top of the iPhone until you see the Apple logo. You can let go then and you should be back in business.

No Sound

There could be several reasons why your iPhone isn't making any sounds. The first thing to check is that you don't have it on Silent. Check the Ring/Silent switch on the left side of the iPhone. Make sure it's pushed towards the front of the iPhone. If you see an orange dot on the switch, that means that it's on Silent. The next thing to check is the volume. Press the Volume Up button on the left side of the iPhone below the Ring/Silent switch. If you're not hearing your media content, then check to make sure the volume is turned up there as well. Lastly, verify that the iPhone doesn't have anything plugged into its headset jack, or if you are using headphones, that they are pressed all the way in. Most headphones will not go all the way down into the iPhone's recessed headset jack. If you have your iPhone docked in an iPod or iPhone speaker system, make sure that the speaker system has power and is on.

Poor Phone Reception

Antenna Area

The iPhone doesn't use an external antenna. However, it does have an internal antenna. It's located near the bottom on the back under the black plastic cover. If you're in an area with weak cell coverage, then you might want to make sure that your hand is not covering that plastic cover.

The iPhone May Cause Interference

If you have other wireless devices in your home/office such as cordless phones, speaker systems, video/audio recording equipment, etc., the iPhone's transceiver could cause audible interference (buzzing) on these devices. If this happens, you can usually cure it by going to Settings (from the Home screen) and turning on Airplane Mode. However, note that while your iPhone is in Airplane mode, you will not be able to make or receive calls or access the Internet.

Turn It Off and Back On

Some problems can be cured by simply turning the iPhone off and back on again. To turn the iPhone off and back on, hold down the Sleep/Wake button on the top of the iPhone. After a few seconds you will get a message that says Slide to Power Off. Go ahead and tap on the red arrow button, then slide your finger across to the right to power off the iPhone. Once the iPhone powers off, you can power it back on by holding down the Sleep/Wake button. Once the iPhone comes back on, you can try to do whatever it was that wasn't working before.

It's Not Responding

In the rare situation that your iPhone is on but not responding to your touch, you can reboot the iPhone. To reboot the iPhone, press-and-hold the Home and Sleep/Wake buttons simultaneously until you see the Apple logo. Then you can let go of these two buttons. The iPhone should boot up normally and return back to normal operation.

Can't Make Calls

In order to make calls, your iPhone has to be active and there has to be a cellular network in range. If you are on AT&T's network, you should see the AT&T icon with your current signal strength next to it. If you're roaming on another provider's network, you should see that network's name. If you don't see a network name or you see No Service, then you will not be able to make calls until you are back in the range of a wireless carrier. Also, if you have traveled outside of your country's home network, you may not be set up for international roaming on your plan. Check with AT&T to make sure that your account has international roaming on it. Also make sure you're not in Airplane mode. If there is a little icon of a plane in the upper-left corner of the screen, then you are in Airplane mode and will not be able to make calls until you turn Airplane mode off in the settings (from the Home screen).

Missing Album Art

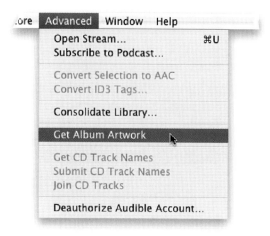

You can download album art for the vast majority of your iTunes Music Library directly in iTunes. You do this by going to the Advanced menu and choosing Get Album Artwork. If you notice a bunch of missing album art in iTunes or on your iPhone, you can correct this by doing the following: In iTunes, select the tracks that are missing album art. Control-click (PC: Right-click) on them and choose Clear Downloaded Artwork. Control-click on them again and choose Get Album Artwork (iTunes will then download the album art for any tracks that you are missing artwork for that iTunes has in its catalog). Finally, re-sync your iPhone.

You're on Wi-Fi, but the iPhone Uses EDGE

This could be caused by a couple of different scenarios. It's possible that you entered your WEP password with a typo. It could also be caused by routers that use MAC address filtering and the MAC address for your iPhone hasn't been entered into the router's filter list. If you experience this problem, first verify that your password has been entered correctly. The easiest way to do this is to go to the Home screen and tap Settings, then tap Wi-Fi. Tap the blue arrow button next to the name of your network. Next, tap Forget This Network. Then try accessing your Wi-Fi network again and re-entering the password. If the WEP password is not being accepted, try entering the HEX key. If your router uses MAC address filtering, then you'll need to log onto your router's admin page and enter the iPhone's Wi-Fi MAC address, which can be found under General on the Settings screen. On the General screen, tap About and scroll down the screen.

Renew Your DHCP Lease Manually

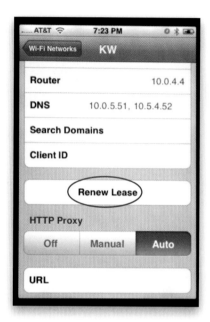

If you're connected to a commercial hot spot, like those at a favorite coffee shop or restaurant, and you're having problems getting out onto the Internet, try renewing your DHCP lease. Tap Settings from the Home screen and then tap Wi-Fi. Next, tap the blue arrow button for the network that you're connected to, scroll down, and tap the Renew Lease button. This will tell the iPhone to grab an updated IP address and possibly updated DNS info.

Battery Saving Tips

The iPhone has an impressive battery life. However, everyone's experience is going to be based upon how they use their iPhone. So there are ways to get a few extra hours out of the battery and to get close to the Apple specs for how long the battery should go between charges. Like anything else, any one of these tips will help, but the more of them you use, the longer your battery will go between charges.

- Try reducing the screen brightness. The iPhone's screen is one of the main sources for drawing power. If you reduce the brightness of the screen, the iPhone will use less battery power. You can do this from the Settings screen.
- Check mail less frequently or manually. Each time your iPhone checks for mail, it has to use the data network or Wi-Fi. Try setting the Auto-Check to a longer interval or turning it off, also from the Settings screen.
- Turn off Wi-Fi and Bluetooth if not needed. If you're in an area that doesn't have Wi-Fi or are traveling on a train, then there is no reason to have the iPhone constantly searching for a network to connect to. Turn off Wi-Fi from the Settings screen. If you're not using a Bluetooth headset, you can turn off Bluetooth too. With these radios off, the iPhone will also charge faster.
- As with most electronic devices that use rechargeable batteries, it's always a good idea to let your battery run completely down occasionally before recharging. Think of it as exorcising the battery and prolonging its life as well.

iPhone Not Seen by iTunes

In order to sync your iPhone to iTunes, you need to have iTunes version 7.3 or higher. If you're a Mac user, you also need to be on Mac OS X 10.4.10 or higher. There needs to be enough battery power for the iPhone to be able to turn on. If the iPhone's battery is completely drained, then you should charge it for at least 10 minutes before attempting to connect/sync it in iTunes. If that doesn't work, try plugging the iPhone into a different USB 2 port on your computer. If you're trying to use it with a USB hub, you may want to see if it works connected directly to your computer first. Try disconnecting other USB devices. If that doesn't work, try turning your iPhone off and back on before connecting to your computer.

SIM Card Not Detected by iPhone

SIM tray

The iPhone is a GSM-based phone and therefore comes with a SIM card already installed in it. If it's not being recognized by the iPhone, try removing it and re-seating it. Using a small paper clip, insert one end of the paper clip in the hole on the SIM tray and press firmly until the SIM tray pops up. Make sure there is no dirt or debris on it and try putting it back in.

---

iTip

If you ever have to send your iPhone in for service, you can remove the SIM card and try it in another GSM-based phone. (This way, you'll still have use of a cell phone while yours is being serviced.) Apple doesn't require your SIM card to service your phone and, as a matter of fact, they request that you remove it before you send it in anyway.

Mac iCal & Address Book Sync Issues

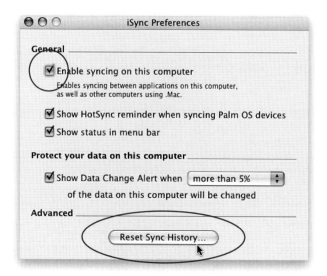

With Mac OS X, the iPhone syncs directly to your contacts in Address Book and your calendars in iCal. If your syncing seems "stuck" and you've waited a decent amount of time with no movement, you may need to reset your sync history in iSync. Before you proceed *I highly recommend* that you back up both your Address Book and iCal files. To back up Address Book, open Address Book and choose Backup Address Book from the File menu. This will make a complete backup file that you can use to revert back to of all your contacts. Open iCal and choose Back Up Database from the File menu to back up your calendars. Once you have both Address Book and iCal backed up, then launch iSync from your Applications folder. Choose Preferences from the iSync menu and then click the Reset Sync History button. This will reset your sync services data on your Mac. Then you can try syncing your iPhone again and it should sync the contacts and calendars successfully.

Get a Fresh Start with Your Information

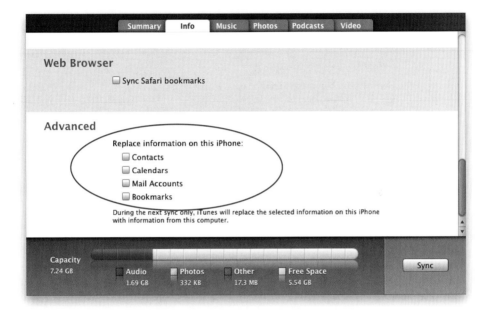

If you want to wipe the Contacts, Calendars, Bookmarks, or Mail Accounts settings from your iPhone and replace them with what's current on your computer, you can do this in iTunes. After you connect your iPhone to your computer, you can choose the Info preferences tab once your iPhone is selected in the Devices list. There is a checkbox for each of the above items that you can turn on to have iTunes overwrite what's currently on the iPhone with the contacts, calendars, bookmarks, or email account settings that are currently on your computer. This will be a one-time thing and will sync normally on each subsequent connection.

Syncing Your iPhone with Entourage (Mac)

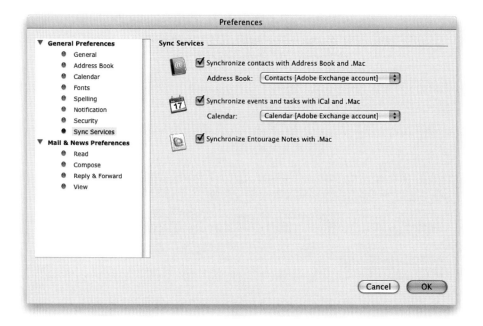

On a Mac, the iPhone only syncs directly with Mac OS X's Address Book, iCal, and your online Yahoo! Address Book. However, you can continue to use Microsoft Entourage as your primary personal information manager (PIM). The trick is that you have to use the latest version of Entourage from Microsoft Office 2004, which has support for Mac OS X Sync Services. To set this up, launch Entourage, go under the Entourage menu, choose Preferences, then go to the Sync Services preferences. Enable syncing for Address Book and Calendar. You will then be prompted on what to do with the first sync. If you don't have anything in Address Book or iCal, you can simply have Entourage overwrite those two with your Entourage contacts and calendar. This will sync all your contacts from Entourage to Address Book and your Entourage calendar will appear in iCal as a new calendar called "Entourage." Please note that it may take several minutes to populate Address Book and iCal if you have lots of information in Entourage. Both the Address Book and iCal applications will continue to sync with Entourage in the background. So if you add entries in either application, they will be synced back to Entourage and vice versa. Now you can sync your iPhone with Address Book and iCal because they will contain your info from Entourage.

Wiping the iPhone Completely

If you want to start completely from scratch on your iPhone and reset it back to its factory defaults, you can do so from the Settings screen. Tap Settings on the iPhone's Home screen, and tap General on the Settings screen. You will see a Reset button. Tap Reset and you will have a choice of Reset All Settings, Erase All Content and Settings, Reset Keyboard Dictionary, and Reset Network Settings. The main two settings that you'll want to choose from are Reset All Settings and Erase All Content and Settings. The first choice (Reset All Settings) will reset all your settings and preferences but leave your data and media intact. So you will still have all your contacts, calendars, songs, etc. The second option (Erase All Content and Settings) is the one that will reset the iPhone back to its factory defaults and wipe out everything you put on it.

Chapter Ten

Setting Me Off

The Ins and Outs of Your iPhone's Settings

 I was a bit concerned about using the song title "Setting Me Off" for this chapter, because I thought it might sound too aggressive for a chapter on something as non-confrontational as learning about which iPhone settings do what. But then when I learned (by doing a quick search in the iTunes Store) that the group that recorded the song was named Speed\Kill/Hate (from their album *Acts of Insanity*), I felt much better about it. Well, that was until I noticed that the iTunes Store people had added an Explicit label beside the song's name (they do this as a warning to parents, because frankly kids couldn't care less. In fact, I imagine that when a teen sees an Explicit label beside a song, to them it means "This is for you!"). Anyway, once I saw that label, I did what any responsible adult would do—I double-clicked on it to hear the free 30-second preview. It was a heavy metal song and I have to be honest with you—I must be getting really old, because I couldn't understand a single word he sang. He could have been reading a *Sopranos* script set to music, containing every four-letter word known to merchant marines, and there is no possible way I would have been able to discern even one. Luckily, my son has a special CD player (generally used only by DJs) that lets you slow the speed of the CD down, and it was only then that I was able to hear the lyrics for the opening verse of "Setting Me Off," which were "Don't go changin'…to try and please me. You never let me down before… oooh, oooh, oooh…oooh, oooooh," so I felt pretty good about it.

Airplane Mode

Although it may be safe to move about the cabin, most airlines forbid you to have your phone (or any other device that transmits) on during flight. However, since the iPhone is more than just a phone, you'll probably want to use its other functions while in the air. Apple has your back on this one. They've included an Airplane mode. While in this mode, the phone, Wi-Fi, and Bluetooth transceivers are turned off. To switch to Airplane mode, tap the Settings button from the Home screen, and then tap on the word OFF next to Airplane Mode at the top to turn Airplane mode on. You'll always know you're in Airplane mode because there will be a little airplane icon in the upper-left corner where the AT&T logo used to be. Once you land, you can turn Airplane mode back off by tapping on the Airplane Mode ON button in the Settings screen to toggle it off.

---

iTip

Although Airplane mode was designed for use on airplanes, it's also useful in other situations, such as being near a P.A. system mic, or during a recording session, or being near your stereo speakers where there may be interference from your GSM-based iPhone. If you start to hear a loud buzzing sound coming from these other sources, it may be your iPhone causing it. Go into Airplane mode to stop it.

Wi-Fi

The iPhone does a great job of seeking out and showing you a list of available wireless networks. By default, Wi-Fi is on. From the Wi-Fi Networks screen (from the Home screen, tap on Settings, then tap on Wi-Fi), you can turn Wi-Fi off or on by tapping on the ON/OFF button. You can also see the available networks that the iPhone sees and may be connected to. If there is a little Lock icon next to the network name, then that network is secured with a password. The iPhone supports both WEP and WPA security. So if you know the password (or HEX key for WEP), you can key it in and log on. If there is a network that you're near that isn't broadcasting its name (it's cloaked), you can tap Other, key in the network name, and choose the type of security the network is using so that you may key in the appropriate password or HEX key. Lastly, there is an Ask to Join Networks button. It's important to know about this one. While you're out and about, there may be lots of Wi-Fi networks in the area. When you go to use the data features of the iPhone, if the iPhone sees an open Wi-Fi network it will ask you to join it rather than using AT&T's EDGE network. Some may find this constant asking annoying. You can disable this so that the iPhone won't prompt you constantly to join networks. However, then it will be up to you to proactively check to see if there is a network available.

iPhone Usage

The Usage screen gives you a one-page summary of your iPhone usage (from the Home screen, tap on Settings, then tap on Usage). It lists the amount of hours and minutes of usage and standby since your last full charge. This is great for tracking battery life. It will also show you your call time and your EDGE network data usage. If you want to start tracking these statistics from scratch, just flick down to the bottom of the screen and tap the Reset Statistics button to start them over again at zero. Your Call Time and EDGE Network Data statistics will be reset. However, your Lifetime call time and battery usage will not be reset.

Choosing and Managing Sounds

The Sounds screen (from the Home screen, tap on Settings, then tap on Sounds) allows you to choose to turn your Vibrate setting on or off. By default, Vibrate is on for both the Silent and Ring modes. So whether you use the external Ring/Silent switch to turn the ringer on or off, the phone will vibrate when you receive a call. You can change the setting for both Silent and Ring independently of each other. You can also change your Ring volume here by dragging the little knob (circle) on the slider with the speakers on both ends. It's here that you also choose a default ringtone. The iPhone's default ringtone is Marimba. However, you can pick from a list of 25 different ringtones by tapping Ringtone. The ringtone you pick is how the iPhone will ring for all incoming calls except those of contacts that you've assigned custom ringtones to. The iPhone makes sounds every time you receive a new voicemail message, text message, email, or calendar alarm. It also makes sounds when you send email and tap on the keyboard. You can turn these sounds on or off individually for each area. For example, while I'm traveling I want to leave my phone on at night for emergency calls from home, but I don't want to hear a sound from every email or text message that comes in. So I turn off the sounds for New Mail and New Text Message before I go to bed. This way the iPhone won't make a sound unless I receive a call.

Adjusting the Brightness

The iPhone screen is very bright and it automatically adjusts the brightness under certain conditions to conserve battery life. However, if you want to manually adjust the brightness, you can. Tap the Brightness button in the Settings screen and drag the slider to the left to make the display dimmer or to the right to make it brighter. You can also disable the Auto-Brightness if you like by tapping on the ON/OFF button.

Changing Your Wallpaper

When you first turn on the iPhone or wake it from sleep, it displays a beautiful picture of the earth. However, if you want to choose a different picture or a picture of your own, you can. Tap the Wallpaper button in the Settings screen. You'll have a choice between the Apple-supplied wallpaper photos in the Wallpaper screen or your own photos that you either took with the iPhone camera or synced from your computer. Navigate any of these screens and choose the photo you want to use as your wallpaper. You'll be able to scale it using two fingers and move it around into position to get it the way you want. Once you have it looking the way you want, tap the Set Wallpaper button.

General Settings

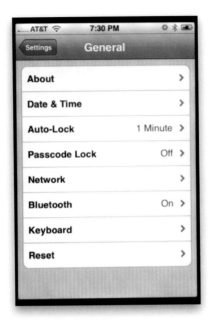

In the General settings screen within Settings there is a lot of useful information. For example, tapping About gives you just about all the information you could use about your iPhone. You'll find things like the number of songs, videos, and photos that you have, as well as the amount of available space, serial number of the iPhone, software version, and firmware version. You'll also find all the MAC addresses for the Wi-Fi and Bluetooth chips. There are some other very useful items in the General settings, as well. You'll find a button to turn Bluetooth on and pair it with your headset, and in the Keyboard screen, you'll be able to turn on the Enable Caps Lock function (boy was I happy to find that one). You can even set up a 4-digit password that would have to be typed in to unlock your iPhone. Lastly, for those needing to set up a VPN (Virtual Private Network) connection to access their corporate network, you would do that on the Network screen. You'll need the VPN settings from your company's IT department. Also note that the iPhone's VPN may not be compatible with your corporate solution.

Don't Forget to Set Your Time Zone

Probably the most important setting choice you'll want to make in the General settings is in the Date & Time screen. Here is where you can not only choose between the standard time display and a 24-hour time display, but you can also choose your time zone. It's important to pick your time zone to insure proper syncing of calendar items from your computer. If you're noticing that the times are off from the entries coming from your computer, then you definitely need to choose your time zone. Tap the Time Zone button and type in the nearest large city in your time zone, and it should display it in the list. Once you see it, tap it and you'll be returned to the Date & Time screen.

Mail Settings

In the Mail settings screen within Settings you can see, change, or add email accounts. However, you can also change the settings for the way the iPhone works with your existing email accounts. For example, here is where you set the interval that the iPhone automatically goes out and checks for new mail. I've chosen every 30 minutes as a happy medium. Although you can set it for every 15 minutes, this will mean that the iPhone has to use more energy to go out over the network more often and therefore will decrease your battery life. By default, the iPhone shows you the 50 most recent messages. You can change this to 25, 75, 100, or 200. The iPhone shows you the first two lines of the incoming message without having to open the message. You can change it from 0 to 5 lines. You can also choose your minimum font size here. This is important for those that have a hard time reading the smaller screen of the iPhone. You can turn on Show To/Cc Label of your incoming messages, which will put a little To or CC in front of your name to let you know if the message was sent to you or your were just CC'd on it. When you delete a message on the iPhone, it does it immediately. However, if you'd like a warning you can turn on the Ask Before Deleting button. If you want to have Mail always CC you on your outgoing messages, you can turn on Always Cc Myself. The iPhone puts a cool "Sent from my iPhone" at the end of every message that you send out. You can edit this to say whatever you like by tapping the Signature button. Lastly, if you have more than one email account set up, you can choose a default email account for sending from other applications.

Phone Settings

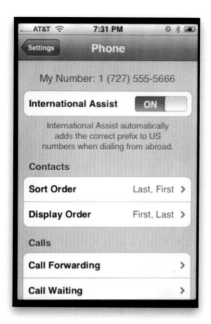

The first option in the Phone settings screen is pretty cool! Since the iPhone is a GSM-based phone, that means that it works in other countries (make sure you call AT&T before you go abroad to have this enabled on your account). I recently visited Australia and the first thing people wanted to do when we got off the plane was call home to let loved ones know that they had made it. The hardest thing to figure out on their phones was what they needed to dial to call back to the States. The iPhone has a feature called International Assist that's on by default. This will automatically add the appropriate numbers to your calls back to the U.S. You'll also find the ability to change the sort order of your All Contacts list from Last, First to First, Last. By default, the iPhone sorts your contacts by last name, although you still see them as first name, last name. You can switch it to First, Last so that they are sorted by first name. Most times, first names are easier to remember. Under the Calls section, you can enable Call Forwarding to have your incoming calls automatically forwarded to another number. Call Waiting can be turned off so that if you're on a call and another call comes in, it will be sent to voicemail immediately. You can also turn off the Show My Caller ID feature. However, keep in mind that many people don't accept calls from numbers that are blocked. Lastly, for the hearing impaired you can turn on the TTY (Teletypewriter) feature. Apple does sell an iPhone TTY adapter separately that allows you to connect your iPhone to teletype machines.

Safari Settings

Using the Safari settings screen, you can change your default search engine. If you prefer Yahoo search over Google search, you can change that here. By default, the iPhone has JavaScript, Plug-Ins, and Block Pop-Ups on. You can turn each of these off if you need to. The iPhone's Safari Web browser is also set to accept cookies from visited sites. Other than Never, this is probably the safest setting. Cookies are good in the fact that they minimize the need on many sites to have to constantly log in. Your login info or site set-tings can be stored as a cookie right in your iPhone's Safari browser. Lastly, in the Safari settings, you can choose to clear your browsing history, Clear Cookies, and Clear Cache to basically remove any trace of your having been to the sites you've been to.

iPod Settings

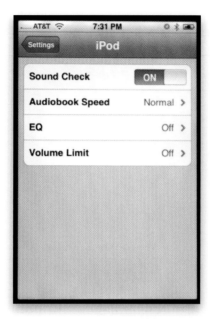

There are four iPod settings to choose from in the iPod settings screen: The first one is Sound Check. With Sound Check on, the iPod application of the iPhone attempts to balance the sound levels of your songs. So, for example, if you have one song that is really loud and another song that isn't so loud, with Sound Check on it should lower the volume of the really loud song and raise the volume of the song that isn't so loud. The next setting is for your audiobook speed. If you prefer to speed up or slow down your audiobook playback, you can change the default from Normal to Faster or Slower. The third setting is for EQ (equalizer). It's possible and recommended to set the EQ setting for each of your songs in iTunes. You can set all your rock tracks to the Rock EQ setting, all your R&B to the R&B EQ setting, all your jazz to the Jazz EQ setting, etc. When they are played on the iPod/iPhone, they'll sound better. You can also set a default EQ setting for the songs that don't have an EQ setting. You can only pick one, so pick the one that would cover the bulk of your music collection. Lastly, you can set a volume limit. This can help those who are concerned that they may suffer hearing loss if the music is too loud. This will limit the volume across the board and there's even a 4-digit security code that you can assign to it so that your teenager can't go back in and just turn it off.

Setting Your Options for the Photos Application

There are four basic settings for the Photos application. The first setting allows you to set the duration for each photo during your slide shows. The default is 3 seconds and you can set it from 2 to 20 seconds. The next setting lets you choose your default slide transition. You can choose between Cube, Dissolve (the default), Ripple, Wipe Across, and Wipe Down. The third option is Repeat. By default, this is off, which means that your slide show will stop after the last slide. You can turn on Repeat so that it loops the slide show. The last option is Shuffle, which is off by default. With Shuffle on, your slide shows will play in a random order.

Index

Symbols

+ (plus sign) button, 28
– (minus sign) button, 35

A

AC power adapter, 7
accessories, 21
Accounts screen, 77
Add Call button, 44, 49
Add Contact button, 27
Add Event screen, 118
Address Bar, 81, 91
Address Book application, 24, 188
Adobe Creative Suite Video Podcast, 147
Adobe Photoshop Album, 160
Adobe Photoshop Elements, 160
Airplane mode, 11
    calling problems and, 181
    interference issues and, 152, 178
    situations for using, 194
AirPort utility, 174
Alarm screen, 103
albums
    art displayed from, 135, 146
    downloading missing art for, 182
    playing songs from, 145
Alert button, 118
All Contacts list, 29
Answer button, 20
answering calls, 20
antenna, 26, 177
Apple Stereo Headset, 16
artist, playback by, 139
Ask to Join Networks button, 195

Assign Ringtone button, 33
Assign to Contact button, 31
AT&T service plans, 20
attachments, email, 66
audio podcasts, 126, 147
audio settings. *See* sound settings
audiobooks, 149, 205
Auto-Brightness option, 198
auto-complete feature, 13
Auto-Sleep mode, 10

B

Back button, 26
background wallpaper, 170, 199
backing up information, 188
battery
    charging, 7
    conserving, 3, 10, 185
    status icon, 12
    tips for saving, 185
Belkin headphone adapter, 16, 21
blackjack game, 92
Bluetooth headset, 58–59
Bluetooth icon, 11
bookmarks, 68, 83–86
    adding, 84
    deleting, 86
    editing, 85
    map, 108
    replacing, 189
    syncing, 83
    YouTube, 107
Brightness button, 198
browser. *See* Safari Web browser
browsing history, 204
built-in speaker, 9, 135
buttons
    rearranging in iPod application, 154
    See also specific buttons

Y

Z

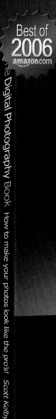